FISHING FOR HAPPINESS

FISHING FOR HAPPINESS

The Ultimate Cheat Sheet To Achieving Happiness And Fulfillment From Top Experts Over The Last 100 Years

Joe Simonds

ISBN: 0692733051
ISBN 13: 9780692733059

Edited By: Ann Maynard
Cover Design: Djordje Grbic

Acknowledgements

To Bruce Downs, for convincing me that reading was cool in my junior year of high school.

To Mrs. Bess, for threatening to fail me in typing class if I didn't learn how to type.

To Ann Maynard, for helping transform my story into a legit book.

To my parents for the endless encouragement, love, and support.

To my brothers, Luke and Daniel, for always having my back.

To my three children, Shauna, Savannah, and Jackson, for the inspiration to write this.

To my wife, Loren, for supporting my wild ideas and for always offering that irresistible smile when I need it.

To God, for miraculously keeping me alive through it all.

Contents

Introduction

1

What I Learned From Spending $100,000+ On Self-Help Books, Courses, and Masterminds

"[Insert inspirational quote here.]"

— Every Self-Help Book Ever

This book exists because I needed to solve a problem: I wasn't happy. I wasn't fulfilled. And I had no idea what to do about it.

Honestly, I wasn't even sure if I was allowed to feel that way. I had gone to school, found a good job, and met a beautiful woman who wanted to spend her life with me as much as I wanted to spend mine with her. We had an amazing house, had a baby, and now I was starting my own business—what could I possibly be unhappy about?

Granted, I had dealt with some pretty awful stuff too. I had cancer, went through some periods of serious alcohol abuse, addictions, some highs and some lows, and even flat-lined on a hospital bed once. But I had come out on the other side each time, usually determined to "live a better life." Sometimes I succeeded, other times I didn't.

And so, through the amazing times and the terrible ones, the unforgettable moments, the job promotions, the life changes, the massive hangovers, and everything in between, I determined that the keys to the happiness and fulfillment I wanted were out there waiting for me. After all, the bookstore shelves, talk shows, podcasts, and blogosphere were full of people who had found it for themselves. They had written books, created courses, and drawn out roadmaps to happiness; their websites were full of "It worked for me" testimonials. Surely I could join the ranks of those who had unlocked the key to true happiness. So I rolled up my sleeves and set to it.

I dove into years of intense work. I read hundreds of books (averaging a minimum one new book a week), listened to audiotapes and podcasts, scrolled through countless blogs and joined online self-help courses. I attended conferences, mastermind groups, and seminars in exotic places. All told, I spent over $100,000 on tapping into the minds of great thinkers and prolific doers. And then I recorded what I found. What helped me, what challenged me, what wasted my time, and why. Think of this book as the ultimate "cheat sheet" to all of the wisdom from some of the best teachers and self-help/personal development gurus of the past 100 years.

If you were to go and buy all of the books that I have curated for you in this book, it would cost you upwards of $3,000—not to mention all the time it would take you to read them. And that doesn't even take into consideration the $100,000+ I have spent on self-help courses, mastermind groups, and doing everything I could to surround myself with happy and successful people, trying to learn anything and everything I could.

The crazy part is that regardless of whether these books were about finding your purpose, becoming a positive thinker, getting rich quick or building wealth slowly, how to become a better speaker, leader, spouse, parent, or entrepreneur, they were all trying to achieve the same outcome:

Happiness and fulfillment.

More than that, all of these resources had a handful of overlapping concepts that appeared time and time again. In fact, everything I learned in my journey boiled down to **FOUR critical, cornerstone pieces**. When combined, the following four cornerstone pieces make up the **four corners of the foundation** that MUST be in place in order for you to have long-term happiness and fulfillment:

1. **Cornerstone #1 - Mission**
2. **Cornerstone #2 - Freedom**
3. **Cornerstone #3 - Love**
4. **Cornerstone #4 - Action**

It's critical to have a foundation in your life before you try shooting for the stars. Just like any sturdy home or building would have a rock-solid foundation before the builders start putting up the walls, your life needs some structure as well. These four cornerstone pieces form the basis of your foundation.

James Altucher described the importance of foundation in his book, *Choose Yourself*, in this way:

> *"Your life is a house. Abundance is the roof. But the foundation and the plumbing need to be in there first or the roof will fall down and the house will be unlivable."*

My goal with this book is to show you what I've learned about these four cornerstone pieces so that you'll be equipped to build your own solid foundation.

Whether you are a college student living on $250 a month, a recent grad brand new to the workforce, a single thirty-something in the city, a parent living in the suburbs, or a multi-millionaire living in a mansion in the hills, the four cornerstones will be the same. By focusing your efforts on these four areas, you will make important choices and changes that lead to a happier life.

I know because it worked for me. It worked for people close to me. And it has worked for people I've only recently met. I've filled this book with our stories.

Now, before we get started, you might be curious as to why I called this book, ***"Fishing For Happiness."***

Can you guess the only thing better than "fishing" for most anglers?

It's **catching.**

Even if we anglers claim that, "a bad day of fishing is still better than a good day in the office," all of us would rather be reeling in a fish than just sitting on a boat all day with nothing to show for it.

Ironically, though, most of us fishermen and fisherwomen spend the vast majority of our time fishing (there's a reason they call it "fishing" and not "catching"). We're hoping that if we spend enough time learning what works, where to drop our line, and perfecting our craft, we will get rewarded with a big fish (and a good story to go with it). In other words, most anglers spend the majority of their fishing careers fishing and not catching.

The comparison is poignantly similar to the way we all hope to "hook into" or "catch" happiness. Sadly, most of us go through life "fishing for happiness" and we get very frustrated when we don't get a bite.

It doesn't have to be this way, and I firmly believe we are not meant to spend our lives unhappy and unfulfilled. We were born to thrive, grow, and live happily. The **Dalai Lama** himself said, *"The purpose of our life is happiness,"* and I couldn't agree more. The great news is that I'll show you how this can happen throughout the book.

A FEW THINGS TO KEEP IN MIND

First, the Bad News: You have to work for it. As Harvard professor and happiness guru Tal Ben-Shahar says in his book **Happier**, there are *"no easy steps to happiness." Having a roadmap might clarify your path from Point A to Point B, but that doesn't mean you don't still have to put one foot in front of the other to get there. Getting what you want takes work, it takes persistence, and it takes action. And that holds true whether you're talking about losing weight, learning French, or leading a happier life."*

You're still going to get knocked down from time to time. Now, just as it is rare that an angler catches fish 100% of the time on every single outing, happiness and fulfillment are not daily guarantees. There will be bad days; there will be setbacks, disappointments, heartbreak, sorrow, and suffering. And there will be instances where it is tough to see the light behind the clouds. It's all part of the deal.

It's a practice. However, with a solid foundation and consistent effort, many anglers will eventually get to the point where they can pretty much catch some fish every single time they hit the water. So, too, will you be able to reach long-term happiness and fulfillment with the right foundation and practice. It doesn't happen overnight, and there is no "quick fix"—believe me, I would've found it. But with practice, creating the right habits, and time, long-term happiness is available to anyone and everyone that is willing to accept it in their life.

Now, the Good News: You can do it! Not only that but the secret to happiness has been boiled down to four easy to understand cornerstone pieces. They are comprised of the overlapping themes that appeared time and time again in the books that proved the most useful, and they will build the foundation for your happier, more fulfilled life. Are there other important areas of your life? Of course. But if you can focus on improving these four things, you will find yourself better equipped to tackle others.

There is no ceiling on happiness and fulfillment! You can continue to raise the bar every year as you find yourself becoming happier and more fulfilled. For instance, I am much happier and fulfilled in my life than I was three years ago, and I plan on being even more so three years from now. And why shouldn't I be? Every year is one step closer to seeing my purpose and my meaning in life met. As long as you never stop growing, you can always move the happiness bar higher.

Also, keep a pen handy. Before you turn the page, get out something to write with and something to write on. It doesn't need to be fancy, and I will never ask you to take pages of notes, so even a single sheet will do. There are a few critical places in the book where you will need to write something down (look for "Action" steps at the end of each of the four main sections). And if you're anything like me, there will be a lot that you catch yourself recording, re-reading, dog-earing, or even posting up on the wall.

Finally, there's the Big Guarantee. If you make it all the way through this book and don't feel that you have a clear blueprint for finding more happiness and fulfillment in your life, then simply email me your name, address, and a receipt of the book purchase and I will personally write you a check for the full amount.

The real reason I put a 100% money-back guarantee on this book is that I believe **ALL** products should come with one. If you buy something from me and don't see value, then I don't deserve to keep your money. End of story.

Here is my personal email in case any of you want to reach out. I can't promise to reply to every email (as I get hundreds per day), but I do promise to read every single one that comes through.

joesimondshappy@gmail.com

Let's get started!

Cornerstone #1

Mission

Mission
Overview

HELEN KELLER was once asked if there was anything worse than being blind. Her answer?

"The only thing worse than being blind is having sight but no vision."

Pretty powerful words.

Sadly, most of us go through life with no vision, no end goal, and no purpose. We are the same people that Helen Keller called out as "lost" decades ago. Many days feel like the same thing over and over again, and if someone were to interrupt us in the middle of our busy day and ask us, "What do you stand for?" we would have no earthly idea how to reply to them.

Let me ask you a few questions.

What do you want people to remember most about you when you die?

What will your legacy be?

Why are you alive?

What is your purpose here on Earth?

Why are you working so hard?

What are you working toward?

Finally, what do you stand for?

I know, I know. They're really tough. You might not have the responses right now—and that's okay—but finding clear answers to these questions is the first step to figuring out how to put all of the other pieces of your life's puzzle together.

As I mentioned earlier, I have spent a lot of money and time in pursuit of my answers. Sometimes it was as simple as pressing *"Place Your Order"* in my ***Amazon Prime*** account; other times, I had to jump through some hoops. For instance, I became a member of the War Room Mastermind so I could be around some of the most successful people in the world. This group only accepts a hundred people at any given time. You're competing with people from as far away as China or Brazil for your spot, and you have to show that you have made at least $1 million in a single year to join (and they charge you $25,000 each year just to be a part of it – they even raised the price higher shortly after I joined). I can safely say it was the single biggest expenditure I've made along this journey of mine. It was worth it, too.

Would you like to know the most important, powerful, and life-changing advice I received in this mastermind group over numerous meetings of hanging with people that make seven, eight, and even nine figures per year? After networking with famous authors, entrepreneurs, and industry leaders, it all boiled down to one BIG idea that made it all worth it.

It was this hard-hitting advice from **Ryan Deiss**, founder of a company called Digital Marketer.

He said: *"Companies don't fail to grow because of websites, locations, people, equipment, stock prices, or any other excuse that dying companies try to blame for their tough times or bad luck.*

"Instead, companies fail to grow when they lose sight of their mission and purpose in the world. They begin to die when they forget about why they were started in the first place. They fail when they forget about their core values, and they collapse when they no longer stand for anything. In other words, they die when they forget what the picture on the front of the puzzle looks like."

What a great insight! And Ryan isn't the only super-successful guy to adhere to this brand of thinking. Rich Devos, the founder of Amway, said the same thing in his book, **Simply Rich**: *"When we started Amway, we thought, "It's okay to start a business to make money, but what's the ultimate purpose of our business? What does it stand for? What's driving it emotionally beyond just trying to make money?"*

Similarly, Simon Sinek's book, **Start With Why**, had to this to say regarding your mission in both your business and personal life: *"Very few people or companies can clearly articulate WHY they do WHAT they do. By WHY I mean your purpose, cause or belief – WHY does your company exist? WHY do you get out of bed every morning? And WHY should anyone care? People don't buy WHAT you do, they buy WHY you do it."*

Ryan Deiss continued to tell our mastermind group that having a clearly defined mission, goals, and core values ensure that every decision you make is in alignment. With no defined mission, core values, or belief system in place, it is incredibly easy to make poor decisions, get off track, and find yourself or your company in dire straits.

As I sat there listening to him talk about how his company had gone through some tough times and was finally back on track thanks to clearly defining their core values, mission, and long-term vision, I realized that this was the missing link in both my business and personal life. I almost wanted to shout it out: the ***exact same theory applies to people***!

My mind immediately connected to one of my favorite books, ***The 7 Habits Of Highly Effective People*** by Stephen Covey. In it, he talks about the importance of a personal mission statement. It was the main focus on his "Habit #2" which states: *"Begin with the end in mind."*

Here is what Stephen said about the power of a personal mission statement:

> *"A personal mission statement focuses on what you want to be and do. It is your plan for success. It reaffirms who you are, puts your goals in focus, and moves your ideas into the real world. Your mission statement makes you the leader of your own life. You create your own destiny and secure the future you envision."*

I don't know about you, but as I read those lines I can't help but think of how SOLID that sounded. Reaffirming who you are—FIRM. Your focused goals—UNWAVERING. Bringing your ideas out of your head and into the world—REAL. A personal mission statement is like the bedrock of a solid foundation! There were three other critical "cornerstone" pieces, but having a mission in place was the main piece of the puzzle. Without a mission, a reason, or a purpose in life, long-term happiness and fulfillment would be almost impossible.

It all started to click together, and it was at this time that I knew without a doubt what the main part of this book on happiness was supposed to revolve around. Without a purpose and mission, nothing else really matters. No amount of money, fame, or earthly desires can lead you to fulfillment if you don't have an end goal and if you don't stand for anything.

The critical importance of having a mission and purpose in your life is a recurring theme in many of the books I read, like Steve Harvey's *Act Like A Success Think Like A Success*, Stephen Cope's, *The Great Work Of Your Life*, which refers to it as your "dharma," James Allen's, *As A Man Thinketh*, which refers to your mission as "your Vision," Simon Sinek's, *Start With Why*, which calls it the "WHY," Amy Tangerine's, *Craft A Life You Love,* which refers to purpose as "defining your CRAFT," and Gary Keller's *The One Thing*, which called your mission—you guessed it— "Your ONE THING." Other books, such as *The Alchemist, The Prophet,* and *The Way Of The Peaceful Warrior*, applied a mythological importance to it.

While listening to Mike Dillard interview author, space pioneer, and innovator, Dr. Peter Diamandis about his book, *Abundance*, I was introduced to an entire new name for having a mission and purpose in life. During the interview, Peter revealed what he believes is the most critical objective to a bold and abundant life… having a clear *MTP*.

What the heck is an MPT? It's a *"Massively Transformative Purpose."* According to Peter, your MPT answers things such as: *"Why are you here on Earth? What is it that wakes you up in the morning, excited for the day? What is it that steals your shower time? What is it that keeps you going until 3o'clock in the morning and fuels you like nothing else in life?"* When you can define your MTP, then you've got a blueprint to find happiness and fulfillment in life.

Jay Abraham even had an entire chapter in his book, *Getting Everything You Can Out Of All You've Got*, that reflects on how critical it is to know what your purpose is in everything you do. It can be summed up in his chapter titled, *"How can you go forward if you don't know which way you're facing?"*

Jay goes on further to say, *"If a child comes to you and says, "I don't feel so good," you respond, "Where does it hurt?" The child tells you where (head, tummy, throat, leg, etc.) and you begin the process of fixing the ailing area. So why don't people do the same thing in their business (and personal) lives?*

Similarly, Tony Robbins summed up the importance of a clearly defined mission with one sentence in his audio program **Unleash The Power Within** by saying; *"It's pretty hard to win a game when you don't know what the goal is."*

I'd argue that it's next to **impossible** (not just *pretty hard*) to win the game of life if you don't know what the goal is.

And so that's where we're going to start. With this first cornerstone known as "Mission", we're going to look at how *"beginning with the end in mind"* can dramatically change your present and future. We'll talk about your goals and how to assess where you are with a life-changing questionnaire; we'll examine how a lack of purpose can literally kill you (!!!) and why your mission, purpose and, yes, your happiness should be something you practice daily, preferably in the morning.

Let's go!

2

Begin With YOUR End In Mind

It was a beautiful spring day in downtown Boston, and I was tucked away in a small hotel conference room with no windows, surrounded by thirty-plus insurance agents and financial advisors all in search of one man's secret.

You could hear all of the small talk immediately silence as that man stepped into the room and started walking up to the front. Every one of us was incredibly excited to be in his presence. We were in awe of his success. He had accomplished incredible things in his career, and many of us came from across the country to hear him share his insight and (we hoped) his formula for success.

Ron Carson is a living legend in the independent financial advisor world. He managed over $2 billion dollars from his office in Omaha, Nebraska, maintaining an amazing track record over the course of his career. He had been the number one advisor at the largest independent financial advisory firm for over a decade.

This guy could move mountains in our eyes, and we were all incredibly excited to have a private afternoon with him to learn some of his secrets. Notepads ready, we waited for him to reveal all of his best sales tactics and bestow his marketing tips upon us. Instead, he threw us a HUGE curveball.

What did he do?

Ron Carson started talking about death. Yep, he led off a sales and marketing speech by telling us to write our own eulogy. I was sitting there saying to myself, "Here I am, after flying all the way from Houston to hear this guy give me his best marketing and sales tips, and he is asking me to prep for my own funeral! The nerve of this guy!" How in the world was this supposed to help me become a better salesman?

In **Heaven Is For Real**, Todd Burpo says, *"In a boxing match, the fighters absorb some vicious blows because they're ready for them. And usually, the knockout punch is the one they didn't see coming."* And that's what was about to happen to me. Because Ron knew something incredibly important that most of us in the room had overlooked. As I begrudgingly followed along in this unexpected eulogy exercise he was putting us through, something in my head finally clicked. It came when Ron asked us to write down the five most important traits or one-word descriptions that we hoped our loved ones would use to describe us at our funeral.

As I wrote my five traits down on the page, my heart started to sink. The ink wasn't even dry yet, and I already knew that if I somehow did die tomorrow, those words wouldn't be the ones spoken of me.

My beautiful wife, Loren, would have nice things to say—I hoped.

My friends would say I was one heck of a fun guy to go drinking with— on the increasingly rare times they saw me.

My neighbors saw a good-looking guy with lots of money, who could (and did) buy every toy he wanted—and that's about it.

I wondered what they might say if they saw the other stuff. That I drank too much at night to help me get that "high" in life that I was craving. That my money controlled me more than anything else in life. I wondered what they'd think if they knew I logged into my Charles Schwab account about seven to ten times a day to check my balance and see how much money my stocks had made or lost.

I was an addict to money, booze, instant gratification, and short-term happiness and I knew it. And this eulogy practice made me realize just how far off I was living compared to where I wanted to be. My head was full of questions that I couldn't answer. Quite honestly, I wasn't sure what I needed in my life to feel more fulfilled. But I did know one thing for certain: If I kept going down the path I was on, I would end up miserable.

THE ACCIDENTAL MISSION STATEMENT

Would you like to know what I wrote down as the five things I wanted my loved ones to remember me for at my funeral?

Family man
Loving
Giving
Funny - brought smiles to people's faces
Dependable and honest

Looking at those words sent a shock through my system. I was only living two of the five. Two and a half at best. I was honest; I was halfway dependable if it served me, and I was pretty darn funny. But I was hardly loving, certainly not giving (unless you count the money I "gave" to Anheuser-Busch or Svedka Vodka every week), and I was not the family man that God had called me to be.

Do you notice what isn't on that list? Being rich or having money not only didn't make the top five, but it also wouldn't have made the top ten list on my eulogy. Money was controlling my life nonetheless. I started asking myself why was I waking up every morning focused only on making more money? Why was I sacrificing relationships, valuable time, and my LIFE for a bigger number on my bank statement?

I hadn't called good friends in over a year. I had missed family member's birthdays. I had pretty much put all of my relationships on the back-burner in pursuit of making more money and looking more "successful" in the eyes of my wife, friends, and neighbors.

I was married to the girl of my dreams, yet wondering why marriage wasn't what I expected it to be. I was making multiple six-figures per year, but wondering why my life wasn't exciting. On paper, I was living a life that I always dreamed of, but I wasn't waking up relaxed, happy, and fulfilled. Nope. I felt poor, and I felt unhappy, and I felt like I could never have enough hours in the day to work and make money.

The good news? I now had the final vision of my ideal life! By writing down just these five traits, I had essentially figured out my mission. Now I just had to reverse-engineer my life, rebuild on a solid foundation, and start living like the person that I really wanted to be!

The "five traits" approach was so simple and workable. Way more so than the previous times I had tried writing out a mission statement before with no luck.

When I read *The 7 Habits Of Highly Successful People* the first time, I tried like crazy to write the detailed mission statement that Stephen Covey recommended, but I never got anywhere with it. It felt so involved, so big, and I became so fixated on the details of what I wanted to achieve and the goals I wanted to accomplish that it left me with little more than a few hollow sentences that didn't really resonate.

In other words, I was too focused and worried about the "how" and the "what" instead of the "why." I kept placing the "how am I going to deliver my purpose to the world," and "what results will I achieve" before the "WHY." In reality, the only way a mission statement truly works is when you start with the why. Once your why is clearly defined, then (and only then), focus on the how and what. As Tony Robbins said during an interview, *"Once your WHY is big and bold enough, you will figure out the how and the what."*

But Ron Carson got me to write my mission statement without me even realizing it.

It was the simplicity of Ron's exercise that finally helped me tap into the clarity I had been looking for all that time. He simplified it down to five things that we want our loved ones to remember us by. Not one hundred, not twenty, and not some long, drawn-out, ten-page mission statement. Just five core values or descriptive words that you want to be remembered by (that can fit in one short paragraph). In doing so, he also got me to think about my mission in terms of who I want to BE, not what I want to DO.

Deepak Chopra had a great quote in **The Happiness Prescription** about this: *"If you could allow your mind to stop participating in the endless pursuit of goals, time would stop. You would experience your being. At that moment, you would realize that "being here" is your rock, your foundation."* It was a relatively easy (though highly significant) mindset shift: It's not what I do; it's who I am. BEING, not DOING. Pa-POW! I started focusing more on how people will remember me when I die, not on how they think of me today.

Once you've got your five traits written down, you now have a blueprint (and a reminder) on how to go about your life on a day-to-day basis. For instance, one of my five words was "Giving." And every time I catch myself being selfish (which happens more often than I care to mention), a little voice in my head reminds me that being selfish is not what I stand for. Here's the trick though: you can't think your way into being the person you want to be. You have to DO the work to get there.

For me, that meant selling my too-big house and getting rid of a lot of my fancy toys and other vanity items. I stopped checking my Schwab account so much and called my friends more. I started pursuing things in life that would actually bring me long-term fulfillment, like making time to spend with my wife.

Hopefully, by now you can begin to see why I think one of the most powerful things to ever do for the present moment is to write out your own eulogy. It has a way of making you see just how close your current life is matching up with what you want it to look like on your last day on Earth. Give it a shot and see for yourself!

My final tip is to not only write them down but to share them with your family. Once you take them public, there is no turning back. With that extra bit of accountability making you walk the walk, you will find that these descriptions start shaping you over time.

It has been six years since I saw Ron Carson speak and I can still vividly recall what I wrote in my eulogy. The irony is that Ron did go on to give some fantastic marketing and sales tips that afternoon, but I can't recall a single one of them today. The only thing that I can remember is his eulogy exercise. It shows you what really matters, huh?

TIME ISN'T PROMISED TO US

Ron Carson wasn't the only guy I'd come across who talked about the importance of beginning with the end in mind. A short, but powerful book I enjoyed was by Phil Gerbyshak called *Make It Great*. He hit the nail on the head with this paragraph:

"What would you change if you knew you had only one day left to live? Would you spend more time at work, pouring over budget figures? Would you read just one more email from a complaining co-worker? Would you

check your voicemail one last time? What would your obituary say about your life? If you knew when the end was, I'd guess you would do all of those things you've been meaning to do, but just never had the time to do. What's stopping you from doing them right now?"

It's a pretty compelling question, right? Thinking about our time as a limited quantity can certainly be motivating. Other authors took an even more direct approach: they straight up told me (or, should I say *reminded* me) that I'm going to die.

The one thing guaranteed in life is Death. Stephen Cope's ***The Great Work Of Your Life*** said this about death:

"Death is inevitable for the living. Since this is inevitable, you should not sorrow. Stand at the center and embrace death with your whole heart. Then your work will last forever."

Knowing that, why not live life to the fullest with our limited time here on Earth? Why not let our 100% guaranteed mortality drive us? Walt Disney has been one of my favorite subjects to study, and I was surprised to learn how much he was driven by his fear of death.

In Pat Williams' book, ***How To Be Like Walt***, he reveals that *"When Walt Disney was in his twenties, a slideshow fortuneteller told him he would die before the age of thirty-five, and that his death would take place near his birthday."*

That fear of dying young stuck with Walt his entire life. Every day he was alive, he worked towards his goal as if he was living on borrowed time.

(It's worth noting that Disney exceeded the fortuneteller's prediction by thirty years...though he did die ten days after his birthday.)

Walt Disney worked toward his mission with an urgency that didn't stop after he celebrated his thirty-fifth birthday. He understood that the length of our timeline is something we'll never know; he saw his time as precious and used it thoughtfully. Pat Williams sums the message up with an amazing quote from the same book:

> *"You are going to die. You don't need a fortuneteller to tell you that. You already know. Life hangs by the slenderest of threads. So you have to ask yourself: What am I doing with the time that remains? Am I using the time God has given me to complete my mission in life? Am I using that time to make my God-given dreams come true? To bring happiness to others? To build meaningful relationships? To build a relationship with the Creator?"*

If you died tomorrow, would you leave this earth knowing that you lived life to the fullest? Would your loved ones remember you as having taken risks and loved with everything you had? Or as someone who went through the motions and never pursued your dreams?

If your answers to those questions are not what you want them to be, what are you going to do to change them?

THERE'S FREEDOM HERE

Finally, I want to talk about the upside of death. I know what you're probably thinking right now—"WHAT??!"—but hear me out because there are a lot of great minds who have talked about this very thing.

When you accept that your death is an inevitability, it is a very freeing thing. Take it from **Steve Jobs**, who said, *"Remembering that you are going to die is the best way I know to avoid the trap of thinking you have something to lose."* He delivered those words to the Stanford University graduating class of 2005. Jobs, the founder and CEO of Apple (and a college dropout himself), was asked to give the best advice he could think of to hundreds of bright young minds, and he chose to talk about death and the freedom that comes with it. He said:

"For the past 33 years, I have looked in the mirror every morning and asked myself: "If today were the last day of my life, would I want to do what I am about to do today? And whenever the answer has been "No" for too many days in a row, I know I need to change something... almost everything - all external expectations, all pride, all fear of embarrassment or failure—these things just fall away in the face of death, leaving only what is truly important."

Talk about clarity! But pay attention to how Steve Jobs says that he has looked in the mirror EVERY MORNING and asked himself whether he would want to do what he's doing if it were the last day of his life. If the answer is no, he keeps track of that. When he realizes that his "No's" are adding up—and they do—he acknowledges that it means it's time for a change and he's *willing* to make it. That's where the freedom part comes in. Jobs has already decided that expectations, pride, fear of embarrassment or failure—the things that "just fall away in the face of death"—don't have the power to restrain him. He's free to live in alignment with his mission, even if doing so means walking away from something great.

Note: It was also **Steve Jobs** that said, *"Being the richest man in the cemetery doesn't matter to me. Going to bed at night saying we've done something wonderful... that's what matters to me."*

All of us have that same freedom to put our mission first and break away from the things that pull us in other directions. And honestly, checking in every day to make sure we're living up to our five key traits sounds like a smart practice. I suggest taking it a step further and asking yourself: If today were the last day of my life, have I been the person I wanted to be? If your "No's" add up, be *willing* to put your mission first and make a change.

The funny thing about "beginning with your end in mind" is that there's no way for us to know what life might throw at us—but don't let that stop you from drawing your blueprint. As Brendon Burchard wrote in *The Motivation Manifesto*, *"Let us decide to take our first steps without knowing how the journey will turn out. If that defines us as reckless and crazy, then let us accept that fate and celebrate the fact that we shall not be cowards. Let us declare: We Shall Advance with Abandon."*

It takes some guts to acknowledge that your time on Earth is limited and then grab the freedom and clarity that comes from that understanding. It's a brave thing to "advance with abandon" toward being the person you want to be remembered as, your mission. I can tell you this, though: you might not know how the journey will turn out, as Burchard says, but it feels so good and fulfilling when you're saying *"Yes"* every morning.

3

The 16 Questions That Can Change Your Life

I PRINTED OFF two sheets in my basement office, walked upstairs to give one copy to my wife, and then hoped and prayed that her responses would match up with mine. If not, we were going to be having a much tougher conversation than just whether we should move to a different city.

I was going through a big change with my business. My role had gone from top sales guy (which I enjoyed) to being the manager of twelve other sales guys (which I hated), to being President of a seven-figure company AND manager of sixteen people, all in one year. And if you have ever run a business, you know that the role of president carries enough stress and job responsibility to keep you busy full-time. It is a miracle I still have any hair left after I look back on all of the stress I was putting on myself during this time.

I spent most of my waking hours in the basement, working on the phone and putting out fires from morning until sundown. I would eat a quick dinner upstairs with my wife and daughter and then head back down to work from eight to eleven pm nearly every single night. Many of these evening work sessions (that usually consisted of me just catching up, replying to emails, and filling out the endless amount of paperwork that goes with dealing with seniors in the financial services industry) were accompanied by a few cold beers or vodka on the rocks. It was the only way I could get through it.

I went from loving what I do to hating it in a short amount of time. It was a shame, but it was also a blessing in disguise as God had much bigger plans for me that I would never have seen if I didn't go through this tough period.

To make a long story short, I finally had to sell the company, walk away from it all, and get out of the role that was drowning me in mental, physical, and emotional stress. Many of the people in my life urged me not to sell, telling me that I had a special thing going that could be worth a fortune one day. But my tank had been running on empty for too long, and despite all of the disappointments I caused with the people I worked with every day (some of my closest friends), I folded and sold. It was one the happiest and saddest days of my career, and I still recall crying tears of joy and sadness the day after it all went official.

Despite the short term pain, I knew it was in the best interest of all parties, and over time I was able to watch all of my friends/co-workers that were ticked off at me go on to reach new highs in their own lives and business.

One of the other blessings that came through this company was meeting a guy by the name of **_Jason Wenk_**. Easily one of the smartest guys that I had ever met in the financial services industry, Jason had a very special gift of being able to visualize and come up with out of the box solutions like nothing I had ever seen before.

Jason also had a story that I resonated with, as he and his family hit a similar dark moment in their life when he and his wife realized they were not living a truly fulfilled life where they were. They created a questionnaire (the one I printed off for my wife and I - that I will be sharing with you in a moment), used it to assess their situation, realized they were not living their ideal life, and took action. Boom, boom, boom. Jason packed up his family in Michigan, drove to Laguna Beach (where they knew no one), and started a new life and new business with renewed energy for his family of four.

For Jason, it all came down to sixteen questions. (Well, technically, he had over twenty questions, but many of them were specifically for his business.) And when Jason and his wife Jillian's answers didn't match up with how they were living, they made the move.

They didn't whine about it anymore, they didn't keep complaining about how they hated the cold Michigan winters, and they didn't mope for years about how nice it would be to move to California. They just did it.

Given how everything worked out for Jason I was both intrigued and terrified when he sent me the worksheet he'd put together. I knew this questionnaire would expose my current life as less than desirable—perhaps even miserable—and that it might show that my wife Loren felt the same way. I knew deep down that if I answered these questions honestly then I was going to have to make some drastic changes.

Loren and I each went to a different room to fill out our sheets so there would be no chance of sharing or cheating. We both agreed that we would answer these with utmost honesty, even if it were the complete opposite of how (or where) we were currently living. No hiding, no cheating, and nothing but honest answers.

After forty minutes, I was done with my questions. I had spent time thinking about and answering each one based on what my heart was telling me. I knew as I was writing down my answers that some things were going to be changing soon as my ideal "core desires" from the questionnaire were certainly not matching up with how I was living in the present.

The big question was how would my wife's answers look. Would they look similar to mine? I sure hoped so. I walked upstairs to see if she was done, but she was still up in our room working away on her questions on her small desk in the corner.

After a full hour of writing, she finally came downstairs smiling, and we both knew the moment of truth was upon us. It felt like a high-stakes card game. All of the money was in the pot, and we were both about to throw down our cards and show our hands. But neither party wanted to go first.

I finally said, "Are you ready to see what changes we need in our life?"

She gave me a smile. "Better now than never," she said with a somewhat worried look on her face. Our high-stakes card game now felt like the moment before opening up Pandora's box.

We took turns reading off our answers to each question. The first two responses were written in an eerily similar way. Praise the Lord! We continued reading off our responses and realized that, although we had pretty similar core desires, we needed to have some serious discussions about making changes to how we were living.

"Well," Loren sighed and looked at me, "What's next?"

THE SIXTEEN QUESTIONS THAT CAN TRANSFORM YOUR LIFE

Would you like to know what the questions were? Well, not only will I share the questionnaire, but I will also share my personal answers. I will also provide a link at the end where you can go to print off a copy for yourself (and your spouse, partner, etc.) This questionnaire was an integral part of a $2,000 online course, and it was worth every penny and more just for what it did in my life. I want to thank Jason Wenk for agreeing to allow me to publish it for the world to take.

Q1: Where would you live if you had no limitations?

"I would live somewhere on the water. Either directly on the beach, on a bay, on a lake, or on a canal with boat access. Someplace warm with lots of sunshine where it never snows. A place with great schools, lots of safe parks, and friendly neighbors. Somewhere that had a family neighborhood look and feel, but still had restaurants and things to do within walking or biking distance."

Q2: Describe your home (size, # of bedrooms and bathrooms, kitchen, living room, great room, home gym, outside surroundings, landscape, pool, near the ocean or mountains, the ambiance, décor of the house, etc.)

"My ideal home would be a newer home (as in not an old historic home – my dust allergies would kill me), two stories, with an open floor plan. We would have 5 bedrooms, 5 bathrooms for our family of five, and a room with a waterfront view for my private office. It would also have a workout room where our entire family could exercise together. A must-have is loads of windows on the main floor overlooking the water that we live on. My home would sit on a minimum ½ - 1 full acre, have a pool for the kids (and me), and have green grass in the fenced-in yard. The views of the water would be breathtaking from the minute you walked in the front door or walked down the steps. The outdoor porch and balcony would be one of the main focal points of the house, and we would eat many meals outside overlooking the water. We would have a large, open kitchen that connects to the large living room where we read, hang out, and play when it's raining. Otherwise, we are outside enjoying the safe neighborhood, amazing yard with pool, and the ocean or lake."

Q3: What time would you wake up and get going?

"I would get up around 5 am, get a jog or walk in, followed by a calisthenics workout and my morning rituals before my girls get up at 6:30."

Q4: What is the first thought in your mind after waking up?

"How blessed I am to have such a beautiful family, to have great friends, that I am not in debt, that I get to live in this amazing home, that my family has great health, and that I know I can positively impact some people today."

Q5: What would you do after getting out of bed?

"Say a quick prayer of gratitude, eat a banana or apple, and then get outside and get my workout in."

Q6: What breakfast would you have? With whom? Where?

"I would eat breakfast every morning with my kids and wife either around the big kitchen table or outside on the veranda overlooking the water."

Q7: What time would you start working?

"I would start working at 8:30 am every day after I dropped off (or walked) at least one of my kids to school."

Q8: When, where, and with whom would you have lunch?

"I would eat lunch at home or at my office either with my wife, my brother (business partner), or an employee."

Q9: What would you talk about over lunch assuming you have it with someone?

"Talk about each other dreams, travel, kids, how we can improve and simplify things in our both our personal and business life."

Q10: How would you spend your evening? With whom and where?

"The evening would be my family. Doing things outside until the sun went down. Either in the pool, walking around the neighborhood, hanging out with friends, or out in the boat fishing. After the sun sets, head back indoors for dinner, showers, reading, and then bed."

Q11: What is your relationship with your spouse (if you are married) and your children?

"Complete love and an open relationship to discuss anything going on in our lives (with my wife). A loving, caring, and guiding relationship with my kids. Never force them into things, but encourage and lead them down the right paths and let their feet do the walking. Teach them right from wrong, teach them to pursue what makes them happy, teach them how to share/give back, and help them learn from their mistakes."

Q12: How would you end your day and what is your last thought before going to bed?

"Kissing my wife goodnight after we pray together. My last thought would be how grateful I am for everything in my life."

Q13: What kind of physical state are you in?

"I'm in peak physical health, lean, and very flexible from exercising for an hour every morning. I can do more pushups and pull-ups than any other point in my life."

Q14: What is your spiritual yearning?

"I want to continue to grow closer to God, to understand the Bible better, and to teach others (starting with my kids) the power of God's word. I want to continue to get better at not being judgmental. I want to impact and bring smiles to as many people as I can with my positive attitude, regardless of skin color, background, religious beliefs, etc."

Q15: What is your relationship with your friends and colleagues?

"Fun, encouraging, and helpful. Always uplifting the people around me and letting them how much I appreciate them in my life."

Q16: What would you do to fulfill your life?

"Start my own charity where I give 10% of my income into it and get to see first-hand how it impacts other people less fortunate than me. Get more involved in Church; get more involved in the community. Public speaking to help encourage others to break out of their shell and pursue their higher calling. Read a new book every week. Travel with my wife and kids."

Go to www.joesimonds.com/core-desires-worksheet to get a PDF version of this to print for you, your spouse, parents, kids, or anyone else you think could use it in their lives.

WHAT'S NEXT?

So you might be wondering what Loren and I did after we compared all of our answers.

Well, that evening we both decided we needed to move. After comparing our answers, we realized that several of our core desires were aligned in crystal-clear ways—and they weren't being met. We didn't live on or near the water. We didn't have our dream house (although our home was pretty sweet). We weren't in our dream neighborhood either. We weren't in the best shape of our lives, and we were barely accomplishing the spiritual and relationship goals we had written down.

We discussed a few places, and after some healthy debate, we decided Tampa, Florida, would be the ideal spot. It was sunny, it was warm, there was plenty of water to live on, the school systems were great there, my brother Luke (who's also my business partner) lives in Tampa, and it was close to my parents and youngest brother Daniel, who live in Winter Haven.

Step two was writing down our goals. We took this questionnaire in January of 2014 and wrote down (and signed our names to it) that we would be living in Tampa, Florida, with new jobs sometime during or before 2016. That gave us time to line up jobs, get a plan together for our girls regarding school, and prep for the long-distance move.

After visiting the area a few times, we decided that a house on the water or canal on Harbour Island or Davis Island (two islands near downtown Tampa) was the exact backdrop that we both described in our core desires. So that evening I wrote down "Davis Island 2016" on a big sheet of paper that I kept on my desk and looked at every day from then.

Once we wrote it down and made it a priority, things happened quicker than we planned. Every morning, Loren and I would ask ourselves, "Why keep waiting until 2016? We just admitted we aren't happy." Finally, we said, "Let's just do this."

So I started the process of selling my new company, and my wife started the process of quitting her job, we gave away thousands of dollars worth of furniture, clothes, and accessories that we didn't need, and we made the move to Tampa seven months early in May of 2015.

SEEING IS BELIEVING

It's funny how a **written goal** that you focus on daily can lead to action so much quicker than a dream kept in your head.

If you take anything from this chapter, let it be that writing out your answers to the questionnaire is an essential step, as it writing down any conclusions you reach. Put your written goals, intentions, desires (or whatever you choose to call them) somewhere you can see them and stare at them every morning. And then read them while *firmly believing* that you will accomplish them.

John Gray said this about the power of knowing what you want and setting your intentions in his book, ***How To Get What You Want And Want What You Have***:

> *"By setting your intentions, automatically things start coming to you. Right away, you get to see the creative power of thoughts. By setting your intentions, you are creating your day."*

The book, ***The Magic Power Of Thinking Big*** by David Schwartz has one of my favorite quotes on goals:

> *"A goal is an objective, a purpose. A goal is more than a dream: it's a dream being acted upon. A goal is more than a hazy, "Oh, I wish I could. A goal is a clear "This is what I'm working toward." Nothing happens, no forward steps are taken, until a goal is established."*

Top-selling author Harvey Mackay even had an entire chapter of his book, ***Swim With The Sharks***, called, *"If you don't have a destination, you'll never get there."*

I am happy to report that we have lived in Tampa for a little over one year (as of this writing), we are more fulfilled in our lives than ever, and

Loren and I have a plan for our dream home on the (salt)water that we hope and pray will happen soon. But the first step was moving closer to where we knew we should be, to stop making excuses and to just do it!

Some of it was tough, of course. Moving to another state meant leaving behind good friends and all the little things we loved about our town. It meant uprooting our girls and finding new jobs and, yeah, it felt a bit daunting at times. But I took comfort in knowing that you usually have to give up something to advance in life. Mike Hernacki says it plain and simple in his book, ***The Ultimate Secret To Getting Everything You Want***, when he says, *"You must be willing to give up something in order to get something."* We just kept reminding ourselves that it would be worth it.

It's important to note that goals can be achieved in steps, as each step creates more excitement and fulfillment. I'm happy to report that I have never seen my wife so excited about where we are in our lives. Even though we aren't in our ideal home yet, we often look at our next home (as in we literally go and stare at one of the two homes we know we will be moving next). And while it might sound wacky to regularly stare at our future home, Loren and I view it as looking into our future. As David Schwartz said in The Magic Power Of Thinking Big, *"Look at things not as they are, but as they can be. Visualization adds value to everything. A big thinker always visualizes what can be done in the future. He isn't stuck with the present."*

The one final point I want to make about this is to set a goal and work towards it. As I have found in life, good ideas and dreams are a dime a dozen. Everyone has ideas, yet few take action on them. There is NOTHING keeping you from moving, from upgrading, from downgrading, or whatever it is your core desires questionnaire spells out. Nothing. Make a plan, write down the goal, and make your move to find happiness.

It's one thing to think BIG or know what you want in life, but it's another thing to write down your goals and dreams, have your spouse do the same thing, and then strive to hit the goals together. Pretty powerful stuff when you involve other loved ones in your life's mission.

As Napoleon Hill famously said in his book, **Think And Grow Rich**, *"Desire is the starting point of all achievement and the first step towards riches,"* followed by if you want to create anything in life, you have to *"write out a clear, concise statement"* of whatever it is you are trying to achieve. *"The point is clear,"* says David Schwartz in **The Magic Power of Thinking Big**, *"People who get things done in this world don't wait for the spirit to move them; they move the spirit."* You will hit any realistic goal you set in life if you believe in them and have a burning desire to see it through, and "move the spirit" yourself.

Pa-POW!

4

Find Your Ikigai (The Reason You Wake Up In The Morning)

FOR MOST OF my career in the financial services industry, I would daydream about retirement. I would dream about my last day at work and how happy I would be when I could finally retire and sit on a beach with a cold drink in hand.

For one, I didn't really love my job, so I savored the thoughts of being able to finally say goodbye and live the retired life. It was no stretch to assume I'd be happier sitting on a beach or on a boat with a fishing rod than I would be at work.

Secondly, I worked in the retirement income space and spent most of my day creating lifetime income for people who were about to retire from their careers. I'd say ninety percent of the soon-to-be retirees that came across my desk had attempted to follow the same popular (but severely flawed) model for life:

- Work hard. Study hard. Be good. Don't color outside the lines.
- Graduate high school.
- Go to college no matter how much it costs.
- Land your first job or go back to school for another degree.

- Continue to work hard even if you hate your job.
- Kiss your boss's butt.
- Get promoted.
- Save ten percent of your income each year.
- Get married.
- Have kids.
- Retire at age sixty-five with a seven-figure retirement account.
- Sail off on your dream retirement. Go travel or put your feet in the sand.
- Never have a worry again. Your retirement will be stress-free and amazing!
- Do all of this, and you will *eventually* be happy.

Sounds pretty awesome on paper, doesn't it? It's no wonder we've been fooled by this false perception of retirement. Let me ask you a question. How many people do you know that have actually accomplished this list above? And I'm talking about every single step (including the stress-free and happy part). I can tell you I don't know a single one. Yet, that is what all of the marketing brochures, retirement commercials, and anyone else who wants to sell you something will tell you retirement looks like.

These steps were also what many of our parents and schools taught us to do. Stay within the lines. Don't take big risks. Keep saving and putting some money into your 401(k) and you should have enough to retire on if you are consistent for long enough. And *eventually*, you will be stress-free and happy. Hogwash!

I can write an entire book about what I saw behind the scenes in the real retirement world, where the majority of 65-year-olds are crippled with stress, bad debt, and realizing they don't have enough money to last them the rest of their life. Talk about a wake-up call.

There are a lot of ways in which the realities of retirement can derail your happiness, and several of them have nothing to do with money. They are something completely different… something even scarier.

We were visiting my parents in Winter Haven, Florida one weekend, and while my wife and kids slept in, I decided to take an early morning walk around their neighborhood. I like to listen to podcasts while I walk or ride my bike, and that morning I was listening to a podcast called *"Self Made Man"* with Mike Dillard. Mike was interviewing a guy by the name of Neil Pasricha who was talking about some controversial material in his new book, ***The Happiness Equation***.

It turns out, the most contentious piece of his book on happiness was a section where he suggested that NO ONE should ever retire. To drive his point home, Neil told the story of his guidance counselor, Mr. Wilson:

"The funny thing is that when Mr. Wilson retired, he didn't look happy. None of us did. We had the big celebration with cake, music from the band, and teary speeches from former students. Mr. Wilson said he was excited to be retiring, but his thin smile and wet eyes said the opposite. But mandatory retirement came at age sixty-five… and so he retired. The next week he had a heart attack and died."

Neil followed up this story with several others that followed the same pattern. The stories were sad, but to me, it seemed more likely that the outcomes were coincidence rather than the cause-and-effect Neil was suggesting.

But then he talked about an island in Asia that had more healthy hundred-year-olds than any other place in the world. They live an average of seven years longer than Americans, and they have the longest disability-free life expectancy in the world. Can you guess what made this community so different?

These folks never retired. They didn't even have a word for "retirement" in their vocabulary so they couldn't even describe the act of retiring. The citizens of this community had no concept of it at all!

As you can imagine, they continued working well into their eighties, nineties, and even past their hundredth birthday and beyond. One man was still practicing karate at age 102! Neil went on to say that this community in Japan had one word that took the place of our word retirement: *ikigai*, which roughly means, *"The reason you wake up in the morning."*

Pa-POW! As I got back to my parents' place, I opened up my laptop, went to Amazon, and bought *The Happiness Equation* to see what else Neil had to say about retirement and happiness.

While I waited for the book to arrive, I started doing some research on the correlation between retiring and death. What I found shocked me!

One of the first articles I read was published on WebMD.com in association with the *British Medical Journal* regarding a study of Shell employees that retired early at age fifty-five. Guess what they found in this study? Fifty-five-year-old retirees die sooner than sixty-five-year-old retirees! In fact, people who retire in their fifties were eighty-nine percent more likely to die in the ten years after retirement than those who retire at age sixty. Holy smokes!

I then read about legendary football coach Bear Bryant dying from a fatal heart attack just a month after retiring from his last football game, and Penn State coach Joe Paterno who died shortly after he was fired. Ironically, Paterno was on record for saying to sportscaster Brent Musberger, *"I'm afraid I will die if I ever step away from the game."*

A hard-hitting article in Forbes by *Robert Laura* explained the seven reasons people either die or become unhappy and unfulfilled shortly after they retire. Reason number seven said it all: *"On the day you finally retire, you lose the very identity you spent years creating in the workplace."* For most of us, that could be 40+ years of hard work, achievements, promotions, and relationships that all go away and lose meaning after you retire. What a buzzkill!

A few days later, **The Happiness Equation** arrived at my door, and I jumped right into it. About ninety pages in, Neil starts hammering away at all of the reasons that you should never retire if you want to live longer and live happier.

I was shocked to find out the word "retirement" didn't even exist until the Germans made it up in 1889. They created the world's first "retirement system" as a way to free up jobs and give the older folks a few government bucks during their final years on earth. Germany declared the retirement age at 65 because the average life expectancy was 67 at the time (so Germany would only have to pay out two years of "retirement" on average). Today, we still use that antiquated retirement number even though the average life expectancy is getting closer to 85. Thanks a lot, Germany!

The other eye-opening piece of Neil's slam on retirement was a report by **Fortune** magazine that said, *"the two most dangerous years of our lives are the year we are born and the year we retire."* Wow.

And Neil absolutely nailed it when he explained his three reasons why the concept of retirement is broken. Neil says retirement is dead because it is based on these three assumptions that are no longer (or ever were) true:

1. That we enjoy doing nothing instead of being productive.
2. That we can afford to live well while earning no money for decades.
3. That we can afford to pay others to earn no money for decades (Social Security, healthcare, and other retirement entitlement programs).

The Happiness Equation was an excellent reminder that if your main goal in life is to work hard and save enough money for retirement, that you might be incredibly let down when you realize the pot at the end of the rainbow is empty—and it certainly will hurt your chances of living a happy and fulfilled life.

Here are three reasons that I believe you should never actually "retire" and do nothing if you plan on being fulfilled:

1. Retirement is bad for your health!

A 2013 report by the London-based Institute of Economic Affairs found that retirement increases the chances of suffering from depression by forty perfect, and it increases the probability of having at least one diagnosed physical ailment by sixty percent! Not to mention, the likelihood of becoming addicted and abusing alcohol and other drugs actually increases in retirement.

2. "When you're through changing, you're through."

What a tremendous quote from Pulitzer Prize winner and *New York Times* columnist **William Safire**. It was given to him as advice by famous ad man **Bruce Barton** on why it is so critical to keep working and expanding your mind for as long as you live. Your body might stick around for some time, but if your mind and brain begin to atrophy from lack of use, your body will eventually follow suit. Said another way, "If you aren't growing, you're dying!"

3. Without a proper "Foundation" in place, retiring will most likely leave you feeling lonely, unfulfilled, and feeling like you are on a boat with no rudder.

The problem with most of these people that either became less happy or *died* shortly after retiring is that they didn't have a foundation for happiness in place. They didn't have a purpose driving their lives any longer.

They had let work consume the majority of their life (because that is what we were all told would make us happy). Sadly, by following bad advice of just working hard and saving for forty years meant that their entire existence was tied solely to their job, and they no longer had that outlet for happiness.

Don't let this happen to you. Find a purpose. Build your foundation using the four cornerstones. Vacation more. Find a way to keep working and building something long after you retire so you can live a meaningful life long after age 65—And do it now! Take Tony Hale's words to heart:

"If you're not practicing contentment and happiness where you are, you're not going to be content or happy when you get what you want."

One more thing: Don't confuse retirement with just your job. Retirement in your work is one thing, retirement from life is another.

Teddy Roosevelt nailed it with this quote, *"The best prize that life has to offer is the chance to work hard at work worth doing."* I believe this holds true whether you're twenty or eighty. It's about finding your *ikigai*, your reason for waking up in the morning. It's about finding your PURPOSE and never retiring from it.

And as Neil Pasricha pointed out in ***The Happiness Equation***, your *ikigai* can be anything: *"In Okinawa there is a 102-year-old karate master whose ikigai is to carry forth his martial art, a 100-year-old fisherman whose ikigai is to feed his family, a 102-year-old woman whose ikigai is to hold her great-great-great-granddaughter."*

Lying on a beach and drinking a daiquiri sounds good in the short term—and it is. Who doesn't love vacation?! But if your life is not backed by purpose and an unwavering mission, it'll likely do more harm than good over the long run (And I don't just mean to your liver.)

The Happiness Equation offers the perfect rebuttal to that do-nothing retirement fantasy: *"Work gives us purpose, belonging, and direction. Retirement plucks us out of the spinning gears of the world and drops our withered bones off at the beach."* I think it's a spot-on warning. And you know what the cool thing is? We have a choice in the matter. Teddy Roosevelt's words remind us of that very thing: *"We must all either wear out or rust out, every one of us. My choice is to wear out."*

Having a clear purpose and a mission is so essential to the overall foundation for happiness and fulfillment in life—it's the #1 most critical overlapping theme I found time and time again in all of my studies and conversations with thought leaders—and there's no reason to wait to start working on your *ikigai*. I'm willing to bet that you already have a sense of what it might be, too. "Finding your purpose" has been repackaged and sold as this challenging and lofty goal when I believe it's far simpler than we admit. Take a cue from **The Happiness Equation** and think of what "the reason you wake up in the morning" might be. As we learned from the community of thriving centenarians Neil Pasricha wrote about, purposeful work can keep you alive, happy, and fulfilled for a long time.

Let me share with you an *ikigai* that actually went "viral" on the Internet as I was writing this book. Tim Tebow, the ex-pro football player who's now pursuing a role in Major League Baseball, was asked by a reporter how stressful sports can be (Tim was in a slump and fighting for a position with the New York Mets). Here was his response to the reporter:

"Sports. Yeah, we can pursue it, we can give so much of our time, our energy, and our effort to it, but at the end of the day, I know that's not why I'm here. That's not my biggest purpose, it's not my biggest calling. It's not how I want to be known in my life; it's not as a football player, or as a baseball player... even though I'm someone that has worked hard to accomplish those things. I want my life to be so much more than that. I want to be someone that was known for bringing faith, hope, and love to

those needing a brighter day in their darkest hour of need. And that is something that is a life calling for me, so it's SO much bigger than sports."

Bringing faith, hope, and love to those needing a brighter day in their darkest hour of need.

Wow.

This is Tim Tebow's entire mission and purpose in life. His *ikigai*. His reason for being. Notice how it doesn't cost him any money to do that. Notice how it's something that pretty much anyone can do. This simple yet powerful sentence is what guides Tim's decisions, what inspires him to greatness, and what motivates him into action.

What's your ikigai?

5

This Daily Ritual Can Make You Happier & Give You More Energy

"You are going to make me late to the office!" my wife snarled at me.

"Well, if you hadn't spent forty-five minutes in the shower, maybe you could have helped me get the baby ready this morning," I snapped back at her.

We were at it again. Like two kids bickering and calling each other names over an old piece of Halloween candy, Loren and I were fighting about why the other person hadn't packed our daughter's lunch box yet.

"Are you serious? Do you realize how much I do around here cleaning up after the three of you every night while the girls sleep and you read? I don't want to hear it!" she yelled back.

Our kitchen went silent when we heard our daughter Shauna making her way downstairs. I can't remember which one of us made the lunch.

Seventeen awkward and angry minutes later, my wife opened the garage door, threw her bag onto the passenger seat as fast as she could, and wrestled our oldest daughter into her car seat—"Honey, I need you to stop moving your arms!"

I attempted a feeble, "Have a good day, girls," but Loren was too rushed, stressed out, and mad at me to reply. I wish I could say this was the first time we'd had this kind of morning.

Does this story sound familiar at your house?

A rushed, last minute, and stressful morning. Being late to work *again*. Being late to drop kids off *again*, or late to catch a bus or train. Late to class *again*. Getting angry at complete strangers, or even worse, getting mad at a loved one to start the day.

Well, you're in good company. In fact, I'm willing to bet most of us have been there a time or two (dozen). That story or something similar played out in my house more times than I care to remember. Especially once kids entered the picture.

(In fact, "Can't you take care of it?" and "Why can't you just do this?" are things I never said in my pre-parenting days. Kids take stress and time management to a whole new level!)

As you can imagine, being stressed out, rushed, and angry is no way to start a day. Heck, any of one of those things can get your day started off on the wrong foot, let alone having all three of them hit you over the head in the morning. It's certainly not going to make you feel happy, fulfilled, or empowered to go out and succeed.

Sometimes Loren and I would text each other after a rough morning to say "Love you" or "Sorry I exploded on you." Other days we would get so busy with work that we just let it go and carried the negative mood into our day—usually finding someone or something else to take it out on. **Zig Ziglar** called this passing of negative energy from one person to another "kicking the cat." Ziglar tells the story of Mr. B, a business owner who takes his bad mood out on his sales manager, who then takes his newly acquired bad mood out on his secretary, who yells out at the switchboard operator, who brings her bad mood home to her son, who then kicks a cat. Wouldn't it have been quicker, Ziglar wonders, if Mr. B. had just gone over and kicked that cat himself? The point is that our bad mood can create a ripple effect of negativity that impacts the people around us (and beyond). For all we knew, Loren and I were wrecking other people's day too! Something had to change in our morning ritual.

I tried getting up earlier a few times, and I generally felt pretty good. Loren would do the same thing, and we'd both be off to fantastic days. But we never formed a habit or a ritual to make it stick. Soon, we were back to sleeping in as long as we possibly could before racing off to get the girls ready on time and then face the day (which meant only sleeping in until about 6:45am—still a luxury for the parents of small kids).

When my wife went away for a girls' weekend for a bachelorette party, the last thing I expected was that she'd come home with the answer to our problems.

As Loren unpacked her bag, she began to tell me all about this "life-changing" book her friend Suzy had recommended. "It's called 'The Miracle Morning,' and I think it's exactly what we need!"

Now, I love it when my wife is happy (as any husband should), so I was not going to poo-poo on her joy parade by any means. But having already read a personal development book every week for several years, I had to fight the urge to roll my eyes at the words "life-changing." It's a widely used claim that very few books can deliver. And if this book was so "life-changing," why hadn't I heard of it yet? *There's no way it's this good*, I thought to myself, *but if it makes her happy…* "Well," I said, reaching for my **Amazon Prime app**, "Let's pick up a copy."

"No need," Loren smiled back. "I've already bought one. I'm halfway through it, and it's great." *Well, okay then.*

My next thought was that it would be a miracle if my wife actually finished the book. I promise it wasn't as cynical as it sounds. Sadly, reading had become a hated thing for Loren, thanks to all of the four-hundred-page eye surgery books she had to read multiple times to pass the medical boards. She had all but denounced reading a book for pleasure!

So I simply sat back to see if my wife would finish all of *The Miracle Morning* before I was going to give it any real credit or bother to read it myself. When Loren snapped the book shut and said, "Done," just a few days later, I was shocked! Not only that, but she had taken notes, earmarked pages, and was fired up and ready to take on the world.

And just when I thought there would be no more surprises…

She woke up the next morning an hour early! On purpose!

To top it all off, she was exuberant. You'd think she'd already had three cups of coffee the way she shot out of bed. I still recall walking the girls down the stairs to eat breakfast to the tune of Loren exclaiming at the top of her lungs, "It's a Miracle Morning, Folks!"

The girls and I looked at each other and thought mom had lost her mind. I wasn't sure whether this book was some cult-like positive thinking voodoo or if it really was solid advice. Either way, I was incredibly glad to see Loren in such an energetic mood in the morning. She got the girls off early to school, there was no yelling or stress, and I even got a kiss goodbye as she walked out the door. It was great and all, but I'm also smart enough to know that many of these "personal productivity" books or programs get people excited for a short amount of time, and then they fall right back into the same rut they were in before.

I certainly wasn't rooting against my wife (I loved this new morning energy she had), but I also wanted to keep an eye on it to see how lasting it was. Morning after morning my wife kept waking up early, kept killing us with kindness as we trudged downstairs, and was truly being a delight to be around. But other than that, I didn't see a huge change in MY day. The girls and I kept sleeping in as late as we could (many mornings Loren would come in to jolt us out of bed with her newfound energy), and we still seemed to be running late and feeling a bit stressed and rushed every morning. But none of it appeared to bother Loren like it used to do.

All right, it's time that I read this book for myself to see what it's all about, I thought as I watched my wife dance around the kitchen.

I typically space out my reading a book over a full week's time. That way, I read a little in the morning, a little at night, and finish up over the weekend. But every once in awhile I get so caught up in a book that I can't put it down. Sometimes, I will read all day long and pretty much ignore all urges to do something fun outside, like fish or jog or ride my bike down Bayshore Boulevard. This was one of those books.

I finished **The Miracle Morning** by Hal Elrod in a day and a half. I could instantly see why my wife loved it so much. And many of Hal's revelations about his happiness and productivity matched up exactly to what I believed to be true as well. I decided to give what Hal recommended a try as I knew after reading the book that I (not Loren) was now the only problem in our still somewhat stressful and rushed morning routine.

SIX EASY STEPS TO A MIRACLE MORNING

The morning routine sounded simple enough. It even carried a super-easy-to-remember acronym for the steps: **S.A.V.E.R.S.**

S = Silence. This can mean meditation, prayer, deep breathing—anything you want, really. It's a great way to prep your mind for what will inevitably be a busy, noisy day. **Five minutes.**

A = Affirmations. Typically when I think about affirmations, I picture Saturday Night Live's Stuart Smalley saying, "I'm good enough, I'm smart enough, and doggone it, people like me," into the mirror. But in this case, the affirmations Elrod is talking about are more in line with what *Tony Robbins* refers to as "Targeting." The exercise is way more focused than some loose, feel-good self-compliments. Here, your affirmation consists of 1) what you want, 2) why you want it, 3) the person you're willing to be to make it happen, 4) what you're willing to *do* to make it a reality. It's one heck of a pep talk! **Five Minutes.**

V = Visualization. You can build off of your affirmations here, or even just picture yourself having a great day and getting a bunch of stuff done. The point is to really *see* it as if it's already happened and *feel* how great it's going to be. It's the same trick pro athletes and Olympians use to sink free throws or steer a bobsled. **Five Minutes.**

E = Exercise. Run, walk, lift, do jumping jacks. Get your heart pumping and your blood flowing. **20 Minutes.**

R = Reading. Well, I definitely already had that one covered. Pick a book that is productive and helpful in some way, something you can learn or a new perspective. Personal development or inspirational books are a natural choice for this routine. **20 Minutes.**

S = Scribing. Take a few minutes to write in a journal about whatever is rolling through your brain. It can be anything; the point is just to get your thoughts on the page. It is surprisingly helpful, especially if you're stressing, to pull whatever is racing around your mind out into the real world. One of my favorites things to write about is everything I'm grateful for in my life. **5 Minutes.**

60 MINUTES AND YOU HAVE A MIRACLE MORNING!

The next morning I woke up to my alarm going off a full hour earlier than usual. "This is brutal!" I thought to myself as I slowly rolled out of bed. Of course, Loren was already up and chirpy as usual.

"Going to have a Miracle Morning?" she asked me while I washed my face and tried to wake up my body.

"I suppose so," I said still wondering why I got up an extra hour early.

As I awkwardly went through all six S.A.V.E.R.S. steps (having to reference the book multiple times to make sure I was doing it all right), I realized quickly that some of these six tasks needed more time, while others needed less.

Once I had knocked out my first day, I reckoned that I did feel a bit better about myself. I certainly had more energy when I was waking my girls up, but still wasn't sure why Loren kept yelling, "I'm having a Miracle Morniiiiiiing," as I was 100% sure I never read that anywhere in the book. Nevertheless, I got up early the next day to do it all over again.

HOW MY MORNINGS BECAME MIRACULOUS

The **Silence** step felt awkward. After doing it a few mornings in a row, I realized just how little silence I had in my life. And quite honestly, it was weird sitting there in complete silence in our dark house. (I was getting up at five a.m. well before the sun came up and kept the hallway lights off so the girls could sleep.) But I also realized how peaceful it was. These five minutes of silence, prayer, meditation, and reflection have since become my favorite part of the one-hour process.

Saying or looking at daily **affirmations** was another practice that I had never really done before—at least not on a daily basis—but I quickly realized how critical this step was to the process. By stating your affirmations (which are essentially your goals, dreams, and purpose in life) every day, your subconscious mind begins to start believing these goals, focuses on solving them, and they become part of your DNA. I have all of my affirmations written down, and I read them over and over again during this five-minute step. Do NOT skip this step. It is critical to helping you achieve happiness, success, and fulfillment (and all of your goals).

One of the coolest stories regarding affirmations was from Scott Adams, the creator of the comic strip, **Dilbert**. In Scott's book, "**How To Fail At Almost Everything And Still Win Big**," he reveals that almost every single time he wrote down his affirmation(s) fifteen times a day, the affirmation eventually came true. He tried this strategy on everything from picking stocks, to getting a date with a girl out of his league, to scoring high on the GMAT.

In each scenario, Scott simply wrote out his one sentence affirmation fifteen times every single day. Here is the exact "affirmation" that Scott wrote out fifteen times per day well before **Dilbert** ever saw the light of day:

"I, Scott Adams, will be a famous cartoonist."

Over time, he went from being a complete nobody in the comic/cartoon industry to being one of the most famous cartoonists of our generation. Scott also started consistently writing down the affirmation, *"I, Scott Adams, will be a number one best-selling author"* years before he had ever published a book. Well guess what? His book that I referenced these quotes from hit bestseller on the New York Times list. Pretty powerful stuff.

I'll leave you with one final tip from Scott regarding his success with affirmations. Scott says, *"The pattern I noticed is that the affirmations only worked when I had 100 percent ambiguous desire for success."*

The next five minutes I spend **visualizing** my goals. Let me begin by reciting a quote by *Cherie Carter-Scott* that says it all about the power of visualizing:

"Ordinary people believe only in the possible. Extraordinary people visualize not what is possible or probable, but rather what is impossible. And by visualizing the impossible, they begin to see it as possible."

Wow! Talk about getting you pumped up about the future!

Visualization to me means thinking through and creating mental images of what I need to accomplish that day, while also creating vivid pictures of my future dreams.

One of the best true stories about the power of visualization is from one of my favorite comedy actors, *Jim Carrey*. If you don't know Jim's story, at one point he was working as a janitor with his dad (who was a full-time janitor), and even though Jim was a complete nobody in the entertainment world, he truly believed that he would be a famous actor and comedian one day. So in 1987, he wrote himself a check for ten million dollars and dated it for November 1995 (even though he was dead broke at the time). He looked at it every day and visualized himself being able to cash it in when the time came.

In 1994, Jim was paid ten million dollars for his first major film, "Dumb and Dumber." When Jim's dad died in that same year, Jim tucked the ten-million-dollar check in his dad's breast pocket as they laid him down to rest. Talk about the power of visualization.

If you don't know what you should be visualizing or thinking about during these five minutes, visualize your major goals in life (like the five traits you wrote down that you want people to remember you by when you pass), a burning desire (like your dream job, dream home, or perhaps a charity that you had always dreamed of starting), or some other future outcome that you are striving for (like saving enough to start your dream company, pay for your kid's college, or writing your first book). The most important part is to SEE it happening in your head and dream up every last detail of the event or item.

The next step is to **exercise**. Over the last fourteen years, I have found that I make more money, feel better about myself, and am genuinely happier when I wake up early and get some exercise in before starting the day. Sometimes that means heading to the gym (on days when I extend the "Miracle Morning"), other times it's a quick twenty-minute walk or jog around the neighborhood, or it'll be twenty minutes of pushups and sit-ups, or squeezing in a P90x3 in (the thirty-minute version of P90x).

No matter how you go about it, make sure you incorporate some sort of exercise. Your friends, co-workers, boss, family, and your entire body will thank you for it.

The next step is **reading**. This one doesn't take much explanation. Read a great book, read a newspaper, read up on current events, or read a magazine. Do something that stimulates your brain. Just DO NOT read your emails. That is the not the purpose of this reading exercise.

I always read a book. Many of you are probably wondering how I was able to read a new book every week for so many years. Well, even though I didn't know about this "Miracle Morning" until many years after I started my "binge reading," the act of reading for twenty-thirty minutes a day in the morning is all it takes. What I found was that reading a good book in the morning gets your brain focused on finishing it. Our minds want to complete what we started. And by kicking off the day with a captivating book, I'd get dead set on finishing it. So instead of watching TV at night, I started reading again. On the weekends, instead of sitting in front of a TV and watching college or pro football (besides my teams, the Georgia Tech

Yellow Jackets and the Tampa Bay Buccaneers), I would read. Sometimes I would read with the TV on but muted, and look up every twenty minutes or so to make sure I hadn't missed anything. I would even read on many lunch breaks (Eventually our family decided to completely cut the cord and eliminate TV from our lives).

The final five minutes of the daily ritual is for **scribing (aka journaling or writing)**. Personally, I always thought journals were only for poets, teenage girls, and travel buffs, but I was dead set on following Hal's recommendations, so I finally broke down and started journaling for the first time. It was kind of awkward in the beginning, but after just a week or so of getting into the flow, this became an incredible way to end my hour of power in the morning.

So what should you write?

Write about what you are thankful for your in life. There is something incredibly powerful about writing this down every day. Write about goals you hit or write about anything awesome in your life. Write about new opportunities; write about places you want to travel, write about your family. I never thought I would be a "journal guy," but I am really glad I stuck with this one. It's also pretty cool to have it all documented so that you can go back and read through it one day to recall all of the amazing little things that made you happy in the past.

By Day Three of this new morning ritual, our girls must have thought we were both on drugs. Loren and I would be high-fiving in the kitchen, dancing in front of our girls, working as a team to get them ready, and pretty much doing the exact opposite of what we had done for the prior two years of getting ready in the morning. This book's advice was pretty magical.

It took me a full three weeks of doing it every day to finally start leaping out of bed instead of slowly rolling over and hearing my inner conscience say, "Hit the Snooze, Joe. C'mon, just one more time." At that point, I had finally turned this new morning ritual into a habit (which makes sense, because most new habits take around twenty to thirty days to form according to **The Power Of Habit,** by Charles Duhigg). I was feeling fantastic, I had more energy despite waking up an hour early, and I was getting more done in less time throughout the day. The only downside was that by about nine forty-five p.m., I was D.O.N.E. As in *DONE* for the day where I could hardly keep my eyes open. It felt worth it, though, since I was living on a new high during the daylight hours.

The only thing that didn't work for me was trying to stick too close to The Miracle Morning script. Some mornings I felt compelled to read more than others. Some mornings I had so much energy that I didn't want to stop working out or running. And other mornings I got caught in some powerful thoughts that I didn't want to break free of the silence. There were mornings that I didn't have much time and had to shorten the duration of each step. Sometimes I did it in the afternoon.

None of these things is a dealbreaker, of course. It's still better to do the Miracle Morning steps when and how you can than it is to skip.

Here is what Hal said happened to him after implementing the Miracle Morning in his life:

"My stress levels dropped dramatically. I had more energy, clarity, and focus. I felt genuinely happy, motivated, and inspired. Thoughts of depression were a distant memory. You could say I was back to my old self again—although I was experiencing so much growth, so rapidly, that I was quickly surpassing any version of myself that I had ever been in the past. And with my newfound levels of energy, motivation, clarity, and focus I was able to easily set goals, create strategies, and execute a plan to save my business and increase my income. Less than two months after my first Miracle Morning, my income was not only back to the level it had been at before the economy crashed, it was higher than ever before."

And that makes me think of Zig Ziglar's kicking the cat story again. If you can send out a ripple of negativity, then surely it must work the other way too. By waking up an hour early and doing these six rituals, you get your body going, you get your mind moving, and you set yourself up for success, happiness, and the ability to be laser focused while getting rid of stress. I firmly believe that positivity ripples out into the world. Call it "petting the cat" (or if you are like me – allergic to cats – call it petting the dog).

Almost all of the most successful, most influential, and most results driven people have early mornings in common. From people like Oprah Winfrey to Michael Jordan to Tiger Woods, to almost all of the *"billion-aires, icons, and world-class performers"* that Tim Ferriss interviewed for his book, ***Tools Of Titans***, they all get up very early in the morning and have a ritual they do before most people are up starting their day. Successful (and happy) people avoid the last minute morning rush, they don't wake up scarfing down cereal, yogurt, or a breakfast bar down their throat while running out the door, and they certainly don't spend their mornings stressed out and yelling at their family members.

Finally, as more proof this "Miracle Morning System" works, one of author James Altucher's most popular blog posts is called, ***"How To Be The Luckiest Guy On The Planet In 4 Easy Steps."*** Can you guess what the four steps are?

Here are the four DAILY steps from his widely shared post:

1. *Physical: wake up at 5 am and do 20 minutes of exercise*
2. *Emotional: get rid of all negativity in your life*
3. *Mental: write down ideas, goals, and what you are thankful for*
4. *Spiritual: pray, meditate, forgive, and be grateful*

So you see? Whether you're creating a miracle morning, crafting your mindset, targeting your success, or making yourself into the luckiest guy on the planet, you've got to get started early if you're going to make it happen. As Hal explains, *"Until we dedicate time each day to developing ourselves into the person we need to be to create the life we want, success is always going to be a struggle to attain."*

I'd add that we can't think our way to success, happiness, or fulfillment. There is a second step to making that happen. Let's look at Tony Robbins' insights on action in **Unlimited Power,** where he says: *"Knowledge is only potential power until it comes into the hands of someone who knows how to get himself to take effective action. In fact, the literal definition of the word "power" is "the ability to act."* In other words, the six steps of the Miracle Morning are a practice that we can take each day to bring us one step closer to the things we want.

Put those two together, and you've got a message that completely changed the way I think about my role in this world:

Ideas can inspire us, but if they only live between our ears they don't have any power. It's on each one of us to take action on the ideas that move us, and we've got to do it today, tomorrow, and every day after that until we get what we want. It's not enough to read it. You have to DO it!

Take action every morning. Make your happiness a practice that you do every single day.

Mission
Summary/Action Steps

It took some time and a lot of soul-searching, but I figured out my answers to those tough questions I asked you at the start of this section.

My Mission and Purpose In Life: Bringing happiness, laughter, and inspiration to as many people as I can reach.

This is my WHY. This is the reason I get up in the morning.

I have a secondary mission (that I also have written down) which ties into my main mission statement: Being a loving father, an amazing husband, and making every decision with a family-first mindset. I want to leave a legacy where the world remembers me as someone that brought families closer together, who made children and adults smile and laugh, and who positively impacted millions through my content and public speaking.

Pretty cool, huh?

What's even better is that when you combine your mission, your purpose (or *ikigai*), and your core beliefs (we'll outline how to come up with your core beliefs in just a bit), you will be shocked how quickly the rest of the pieces of the puzzle start falling into place. You will also find it's easier to see the end game and to discard pieces that don't align with your mission, core desires, and beliefs.

Let me share a true story about a mission statement that happened while I was writing this book.

While I was getting all excited about writing this book and sharing with the world what I had discovered, I realized there was one really important person in my life that wasn't truly fulfilled at the time. No matter how much I made her laugh, encouraged her, or tried to get her excited about life, I could tell she wasn't feeling the way that she used to when we first met. It was my wife.

You see, Loren spent her entire adult life preparing to be an eye surgeon. She gave up her twenties to do something that she felt she was called to do. I remember seeing the excitement on her face when she came home after performing her first cataract surgery by herself. In laymen's terms, she gave an old woman her eyesight back (who was very close to being legally blind). It was pretty magical just hearing Loren talk about it. Ever since that day, she knew that she wanted to spend her life giving new vision to people. It was her mission in life, and she was darn good at it.

Just after a year and a half of finally being board certified and doing surgeries all by herself in a real practice, she became disillusioned by much of what she saw in the medical field. She quickly realized that as a result of the issues in our health care system, having a relationship with a client and truly doing what is best for every patient was just about impossible. It had become all about rushing as many people through your office as you possibly could on any given day. How much you billed was all that mattered anymore, and it broke my wife's heart.

Loren was devastated. She had spent hundreds of thousands of dollars on her education, given up weekends for multiple years, given up spending time with our eldest daughter while in residency all to find out that it wasn't what she thought it would be.

After she had quit her six-figure job to move down to Tampa, Loren went back to doing old-school house calls! Yep, my wife started working with women in Tampa on skin care, Botox, and other treatments right in the comfort of their home. And she would spend hours in their house building a relationship and making sure they were thrilled with their transformation. Even though she wasn't performing eye surgeries anymore, she was finally getting to build relationships and see positive changes in people's lives.

But something still wasn't right, and we both knew it. While I was in the process of writing this book, my wife came up to me, sat down across from me at the kitchen table and asked, "So what did you discover was the key to happiness?"

Up until this point, we hadn't discussed much of my findings from the past few years. I shared with her the four cornerstone pieces and then asked her if she knew what her mission in life was.

She stared at the table for a moment, and then said, "I've never really thought about it."

"Let me ask you a question," I said. "If you found out that you had one year left on this earth today, what would you want people to remember you for? More importantly, what would you do for the next twelve months that you are certain would give you happiness and fulfillment?"

My wife sat there in silence looking at me. Then she looked down at the table and started thinking. I sat quietly while she took her time pondering the big question I had just dropped on her.

A minute later she looked me in the eyes and said, "I would do ophthalmology. Having a man or woman coming into my office basically legally blind from severe cataracts and leaving my office being able to see with crystal clear vision is life-changing for them and me. There is nothing more satisfying to me than having the power to give someone sight."

"Well, I think you know what you need to do then," I said.

Minutes later, she was on the computer emailing every ophthalmology group in Tampa to see if they needed a new doctor. By the grace of God, one group needed someone exactly like Loren. Not only that, but it was a fellow female doctor who had made the conscious decision to build a practice where patient relationships and care are the priority (rather than pushing people through the funnel like a factory). In other words, they are all about building relationships and putting the client first. Needless to say, my wife is the happiest I have ever seen her. She found her mission in life, and it is now in full focus. The coolest part is that she landed her dream job within two weeks of defining her mission. It's amazing how the world starts working FOR you once you let it know what you desire.

So what are your mission, purpose, and calling in life?

Author, **Kamal Ravikant** had this to say about finding your purpose (aka "truth in life") in his book, **Live Your Truth**:

"If you ask people what they want, often you get the answer: 'I want to be happy.' But happy is just a biochemical reaction. Neurons firing. Chemicals moving from an axon to dendrite to another. Lightning storms of the mind. Interesting enough, we often feel that something has to happen for us to give ourselves permission to be happy. I think perhaps a better thing to want is fulfillment. A deeper state, one that comes from within, from being your best self. From living life the way you really wish to live it. Then, happiness emanates from within as a byproduct. Naturally.

"And how does one live a fulfilled life? By deciding for themselves what is true - whether it's love, faith, commitment to family, a mission, whatever it is - and then living it... It's that simple. Decide what your truth is. Then live it."

Phil Knight, the founder of Nike, really nailed it in his book, **Shoe Dog,** when he said, *"Don't settle for a job or a profession or even a career. Seek a calling. Even if you don't know what that means, seek it. If you're following your calling, the fatigue will be easier to bear, the disappointments will be fuel, and the highs will be like nothing you've ever felt."*

And **Dr. Wayne Dyer**, in his book, **Wished Fulfilled**, had this amazing quote about happiness:

"Happiness isn't some thing in the material world that can be acquired and stored and used when needed or wanted. If it were, I'd give you a lifetime supply that would guarantee a happy life. No, happiness is an attitude that comes from within you. Happiness is an inner belief that you bring to everyone and everything you undertake, rather than expecting your happiness to come to you from others or from your accomplishments and acquisitions. There is no way to happiness, happiness is the way."

If you knew that you were going to die in one year from now but would still have the same health you do today, what would you pursue that would give you happiness and fulfillment? What could you smile about, be proud of, and reflect on during your final days? For some of you, the answer to this will be incredibly easy, but for most of us, it will take some serious thinking and self-reflection to write one or two sentences that describe our mission and purpose in life.

As I mentioned earlier, there is one other thing that is critical that you have in place that ties into your mission: your core beliefs. Think of it as your "Ten Commandments," or your "Declaration of Being You." It can be anywhere from three to ten different belief sentences that guide your life.

For instance, my top three are:

- Family first.
- Fail forward.
- Integrity and honesty above all else.

Anytime I am making a decision in my life (everything from teaming up with a new business partner all the way to just responding to a Facebook comment), I am guided by these core beliefs. *Family first* ensures that I always put my family above everything else, and it also ensures that I keep my language and demeanor family friendly. *Fail forward* means I should never be afraid to try new things, to take calculated risks, and to become stronger and smarter by learning from my mistakes. *Integrity and honesty* ensure that I don't go down the wrong paths in life, that I stay focused in today's society where endless amounts of smut and unneeded distractions are just a click away, and that I am always honest with myself and others around me.

The other extraordinary thing that occurs when you get your life locked into a defined purpose is that you get more energy. Tons of it. When you wake up with a purpose, you wake up excited about life and ready to take on the day. I used to wake up dreading Mondays (back when I had no purpose and just showed up to spend a day in a cubicle), but now I embrace Mondays and wish I had more workdays in a week so I could get more accomplished towards my mission.

A quote that really hits this newfound energy home is from ***The Power Of Positive Thinking*** by Norman Vincent Peale. Here is what he says:

"You only lose energy when life becomes dull in your mind. The man who is out doing something isn't tired. If you're not getting into good causes, no wonder you're tired. You're disintegrating. You're deteriorating. You're dying on the vine. The more you lose yourself in something bigger than yourself, the more energy you will have. You don't have time to think about yourself and get bogged down in your emotional difficulties."

CAN MY MISSION CHANGE?

One thing that is incredibly important from all of the reading I have done on both personal and business missions is that your mission in life can (and usually will) change over time. Your mission/purpose in life at age thirty will most likely be different than at age sixty. You'll have a different perspective on life, you'll have a different timeline, and your goals and interest will undoubtedly evolve over a thirty-year period. It took me many years of chipping away at the stone, hitting some highs and hitting some lows to finally realize my true calling. And although I don't see my personal mission changing drastically over the next thirty years of my life, I do see it evolving as new doors open.

For instance, my wife's mission today of "helping people see clearer" might evolve into giving underprivileged kids free eye exams after she "retires." She might even open up a free clinic and start changing the eyesight of people that never could afford eye care. Time will tell.

I'll repeat this because I believe that it is important; It's only natural for your mission and purpose in life to change as you mature in age. I really liked a quote on this from the book **Choose Yourself** by James Altucher that said, *"A lot of people say to me, 'I'm twenty-five years old and still have no idea what my purpose in life should be.' When Colonel Sanders* (founder of KFC Chicken) *was twenty-five, he still had yet to be a fireman, a streetcar conductor, a farmer, a steamboat operator, and finally proprietor of a service station, where he sold chicken. The chicken was great and people loved it but he didn't start making real money until he started franchising at the age of sixty-five. That's the age he was when he found his 'purpose' in life."*

It's also important to note that your life's mission and purpose don't necessarily have to match up with what you do for a living. It's great when they do, but let's face it, the vast majority of us will go to work to make money (or stay at home to shape the next generation) and use that money and time to pursue our purpose.

For instance, my dad is in the refractory business. And although he loves nothing more than to see a new incinerator get a clean layer of heat refractory, it isn't his primary mission or purpose in life. For years my dad has received his fulfillment by giving his time and money to other people or groups that need assistance. From giving away money to churches in need to giving his time to kids with disabilities, my dad works his tail off to make a difference in other people's lives. It's what drives him and ultimately makes him incredibly happy.

My uncle, on the other hand, took something that he did for a living and transformed it into his life's purpose. You see, my uncle retired from the Army after many years of serving our country. He's an incredibly smart and hard working guy, so he tried quite a few different corporate jobs once back in the civilian world. However, none of them seemed to "light his fire." After much contemplating and self-reflection, he realized that helping his fellow soldiers transition from the military to the civilian world was his life's calling. He had seen and heard about too many ex-military coming back and not having the confidence or the know-how to get a job, or even worse, committing suicide. Today, my uncle Vince dedicates all of his time to helping men and women in the military get jobs, start their own business, or pursue their dreams with his company Vet Starts.

IN IT FOR THE LONG HAUL

Goals are something *you do*; your mission, purpose, and core desires are something *you live*. They're the things you enjoy striving for every day, and fuel your happiness and fulfillment as you pursue them.

Goals are future-oriented; your mission and purpose are in place to guide you on your journey **every single day**. Eckhart Tolle nailed it with this quote in his top-selling book, ***The Power Of Now***, when he said this about your mission:

"When you are on a journey, it is certainly helpful to know where you are going or at least the general direction in which you are moving, but don't forget: The only thing that is ultimately real about your journey is the step that you are taking at this moment. That's all there ever is.

"Your life's journey has an outer purpose and an inner purpose. The outer purpose is to arrive at your goal or destination, to accomplish what you set out to do, to achieve this or that, which, of course, implies future. But if your destination, or the steps you are going to take in the future, take up so much of your attention that they become more important to you than the step you are taking now, then you completely miss the journey's inner purpose, which has nothing to do with where you are going or what you are doing, but everything to do with how."

Similarly, business philosopher Jim Rohn had this to say regarding the power of goals and being able to lay a proper foundation while never losing sight of "the now" in his book, **7 *Strategies For Wealth & Happiness*:**

"Dreams are wonderful, but they aren't enough. It's not sufficient to have a brilliant painting of the desired result. To erect a magnificent structure one must also have a step-by-step blueprint of how to lay the foundation, support the structure, and so on. And for that we need goals.

Like a well-defined dream, well-defined goals work like magnets. They pull you in their direction. The better you DEFINE them, the better you DESCRIBE them, the harder YOU WORK on achieving them, the stronger THEY PULL.

And believe me when I say that when the "potholes" of life threaten to stall you on the road to your success, you'll need a strong magnet to pull you forward.

Ultimately, happiness is activity with purpose. It's love in practice. It's both a grasp of the obvious and an awe of the mysterious. Yet most of us think of happiness as something either lost in the past or a peak to be arrived at in some distant future (I'll be happy as soon as...). Few understand that happiness can only be experienced in the now."

Goals certainly have their place, though. Once you have your mission and purpose, it is then critical that you write down your five, ten, and twenty-year goals that back up your mission. These goals should have actual deadlines (specific dates that you will accomplish them), and each goal should tie into and reinforce your life's mission. Just as your core beliefs keep you grounded on a day-to-day basis, long-term goals will keep you focused and excited about the impact you can be making in this world.

Let me give you an example of my goals. Notice how they tie in and strengthen my mission that I shared earlier.

My five-year goal is to impact five million people with my message of happiness and the importance of family through my writing and videos.

My ten-year goal is to do public speaking on the topic of happiness, inspiring people to do BIG things in life, and to help bring families closer to together.

My twenty-year goal is to build a family-first theme park centered on fishing, having fun outdoors, and bonding with friends and family. In this tech-based world, there are too many things keeping kids inside—not to mention, too many things tearing families apart. I want my "theme park" to be all about teaching kids about nature, outdoor sports, and conservation of the environment. It might sound crazy, but it is what is driving me today.

The Mission cornerstone can become the blueprint for how you make daily decisions. Think of it as *your very own constitution* that guides you and gives you a plan. It will help you make better decisions about your job, your relationships, and everything else that is important in your life. Combined with the other cornerstones, it will help complete the picture of your life's puzzle, something you can always look at to make sure you get the finished product you desire.

And when you combine a written out mission with an unwavering faith in making it happen, magic begins to appear in your life. Phil Knight ended his book, ***Shoe Dog***, with this awesome quote on faith:

> *"Have faith in yourself, but also have faith in faith. Not faith as others define it. Faith as you define it. Faith as faith defines itself in your heart."*

Here are a few things you should start doing today.

YOUR MISSION ACTION STEPS

Start off by thinking through what makes you happiest. What gives you the biggest sense of fulfillment and energy in life? What are you really good at doing? What is your *ikigai*, *"The reason you wake up in the morning?"*

Then complete the following four exercises (in this order):

1. Write out the 5 traits, words, or short phrases that you want your loved ones to remember you by when you die. This is the easiest way to get your mind flowing on what's truly important to you in life. Keep it simple!
2. Next, write out your Mission Statement. This is the hardest part, but once you can define this, everything else falls into place. Keep it short and simple (something you can easily repeat), and remember that it doesn't have to be some new earth-shattering concept.

Worry about the "how" you are going to accomplish it, and the "what" results you will receive AFTER you create your "WHY."

3. Next, write out your Core Beliefs. These are the 3-10 "Commandments" that reinforce your mission and give you "rules to live by."

4. End by writing out your 5, 10, and 20-year goals. Keep them simple yet very specific.

I'll provide a link below with some great examples of mission statements.

Here are all of my personal answers to these four exercises so you can have a quick reference guide:

MY 5 "LEGACY TRAITS"

- Family man
- Loving
- Giving
- Funny - brought smiles to people's faces
- Dependable and honest

MY MISSION:

Bringing happiness, laughter, and inspiration to as many people as I can reach.

MY CORE DESIRES:

- Family first
- Fail forward
- Integrity and honesty above all else
- Life is short. Always have fun and smile
- Be quick to apologize when wrong

- Be humble no matter what happens in life
- Give back more than I take in with everything
- Fear God through it all

MY GOALS:

My five-year goal is to impact five million people with my message of happiness and the importance of family through my writing and videos.

My ten-year goal is to do public speaking on the topic of happiness, inspiring people to do BIG things in life, and to help bring families closer to together.

My twenty-year goal is to build a family-first theme park centered on fishing, being outdoors, and bonding with friends and family. In this tech-based world, there are too many things keeping kids inside—not to mention, too many things tearing families apart. I want my "theme park" to be all about teaching kids about nature, outdoor sports, and conservation of the environment. It might sound crazy, but it is what is driving me today.

Once you have completed these four exercises (that means they are all written down), share it with a loved one, and read through them once per day during your daily affirmation period.

Next, take ACTION on getting a morning ritual in place like I outlined in chapter 5.

Finally, make sure to honestly answer the 16-questions that I provided you with. I've found that you have better answers to these questions once you have defined your mission, core desires, etc. The website to download a printable PDF of the questionnaire is www.joesimonds.com/core-desires-worksheet

Finally, have **FUN** while pursuing your dreams and goals in life. I love Jon Gordon's quote from his awesome book, ***The Energy Bus,*** on the matter: *"The goal in life is to live young, have fun, and arrive at your final destination as late as possible, with a smile on your face. Have fun and enjoy the ride."*

Make sure to head over to www.joesimonds.com/mission-statement-worksheet for your one-page checklist PDF, and some other tips and examples on creating your mission statement, core beliefs, and goals.

Cornerstone #2

Freedom

Freedom
Overview

It is impossible to be happy and fulfilled in the long run without a sense of freedom and control over your life. Here's the scary thing, though: you might not be aware that you don't have it.

After college, I read a book called *Influence* by Dr. Robert Cialdini, and it opened my eyes to all the ways that animals can be conditioned to perform odd behavior. There were Ivan Pavlov's dogs, of course, and the story of the elephant and the rope. But the story that jumped out the most to me was one about mother turkeys. A study discovered that a mother turkey is triggered to act like a mom all from one thing: the "cheep-cheep" sound of a baby turkey. If a chick makes the noise, its mother will care for it. If it doesn't (or can't), the mother ignores the chick and sometimes even kills it! Crazy!

The researchers went on to further test the extent of the mother turkey's instinct by placing a stuffed replica of the turkey's most natural enemy, the polecat, near the mama gobbler. When they put a stuffed polecat near her, the mother went crazy with anger and starting clawing, pecking, and squawking at the stuffed polecat. Makes sense. But then they took the same stuffed polecat and used a small recorder to play that "cheep-cheep" sound from it. As soon as the mother turkey heard the chirping from the stuffed polecat, she not only accepted her natural enemy but gathered it underneath her to care for it. Wild stuff indeed!

Cialdini goes on to explain how we as humans can be "conditioned" and influenced to do dumb things just as easily as the animals in all of the experiments—why we say yes to things we should turn down or how we make choices depending on what our neighbors do. It's a fascinating book. Of course, I thought I was too smart ever to get manipulated by some stimulus. I didn't know the power of conditioning until it hit me right in between the eyes.

I was on the couch reading Brendon Burchard's **The Motivation Manifesto** while my two little daughters played on the floor next to me. The chapter was a convicting one, as Burchard broke down the way cell phones, text messages, and emails are controlling our lives. He even poked fun at how most of us freak out if we aren't within arm's length of our cell phone at any given time. (Of course, I glanced over to make sure my cell phone was still next to my lap on the couch when I read that—probably like you are doing now.) I finished up the chapter, put the book down next to my phone, and decided to get on the floor to spend some time with girls.

Within two minutes, my phone let out a "DING!" I quickly hopped up from the floor, grabbed my phone to read the text, quickly typed a response, and went back to my girls. Just as I was sitting down next to little baby Savannah, my phone went off again. I hopped back up with lightning speed, skipped over to my phone, and I was off typing away again. I placed the phone back on the couch and settled in for some *quality time* with my girls… again.

"DING!" This time it was an email. One of my co-workers needed some help putting out a small fire.

Now the girls were looking at me. Probably wondering why Dad kept sitting down and then getting up. It couldn't have been more than three minutes after emailing my reply when my phone rang. I figured it was probably my co-worker needing further guidance, so I jolted up to catch the call. While I was talking to him, my three-year-old, Shauna, was tugging on my leg asking me to help her build something with her jumbo-size Legos. I kept holding my index finger up to my lips to let her know that I was on the phone and I needed her to be quiet. If you have spent any time around a persistent three-year-old, you know that the old "give me a minute" or finger-to-mouth "shhh" rarely has any effect.

Shauna kept tugging on my leg as I tried to my best to ignore her while carrying on the conversation on the other end of the phone. Finally, she reached up, grabbed the bottom of my shirt, and said, "Dad, please help me build a train!"

With my frustration level at an all-time-high, I took the phone away from my ear, hit the mute button, and yelled at my beautiful daughter at the top of my lungs, "Would you be quiet? Can't you see that I am on the phone?! What is wrong with you?!!"

As I hit the mute button again to continue the conversation, I could hear Shauna starting to cry. Immediately, I felt like the worst dad ever. I had a daughter that I loved more than anything now screaming hysterically because I had yelled at her over a phone call that could have waited until the next day. My final words to her—"What is wrong with you..."—were still ringing in my ears.

The real question that afternoon was, "What is wrong with ME?"

I think you probably already know the answer: My cell phone was controlling me. I was just as easy to condition as Pavlov's dog. My phone makes a beep, I jump up and grab it. My phone rings, I stop whatever I am doing (even spending quality time with my kids), and answer it. In other words, if my phone makes a noise, I jump. Who is controlling who here?

This is a huge problem, people. Next time you are in a restaurant, look around to see how many people are either on their phone or have it sitting right up on the table, so they don't miss anything. And tons of people even leave their ringers on out in public places! Those alert tones will sound off in important business meetings, during anniversary dinners, movie theatres, and everything in between. Talk about having zero control.

You might not realize it, but when something (anything!) has that much control over you, it is taking away from your happiness. Whether it's a phone, a controlling spouse, a controlling boss, a controlling stomach, a controlling credit card, or a controlling mind, it can take away from your freedom and happiness. Anytime you are a slave to something, the chances of you finding fulfillment grow slim.

For instance, I'm willing to bet you know someone who complains about his or her job non-stop. Ask him or her why they don't look for a new job, and you get a reply with something like, "Well, I've got a family now, and the company I'm with has good health benefits." Or you'll hear, "It could take me months to find a job with the same pay," or "But if I leave now, I could miss out on a potential end of the year bonus." Those reasons may sound valid, but are they worth exchanging your freedom and control?

In *The Motivation Manifesto*, Burchard clearly lays out the importance of having control over your fears, weaknesses, and insecurities in being happy long term when he says, *"Reclaiming our life agenda is about asking, "Am I proud of who I am and the person I am becoming? Am I happy with what I am doing and contributing to the world? Have I felt grateful for this day and its opportunities, and have I directed myself purposefully so that I can live my highest truth and serve my highest good?"*

These are such important questions! But if we're going to answer them truthfully, Brendon reminds us that we must first ask something else:

"Let us boldly ask what it says about ourselves if we cannot pull back from our addiction to digital distractions. For it is an addiction; we are no better off than the alcoholic who cannot avoid the bar or the gambler in the casino…"

That line hit home for me.

The reason that depression rates are at all-time highs today is that so many of us lack control and freedom in our lives. We let technology, our finances, other people's standards of success, and our own fears control us so much that we lose touch with what it feels like to be in the driver's seat of our life. We are hardwired with a burning desire for freedom, and when it is taken away (even by something as small as a cell phone or a sweet tooth), it slowly eats away at your long-term happiness.

Dan Ariely explains how a lack of self-control can negatively impact your life in his book, ***Predictably Irrational***. He has this to say about it:

"When we have problems with self-control, sometimes we delay tasks that we should do immediately (procrastination). But we also exhibit problems with self-control when we attend too frequently to tasks that we should put off—such as obsessively checking our email."

Dan goes on to explain that options distract us from our mission because *"in every case we give something up for those options."* In other words, by giving control over to something or someone else, we are taking a step further away from what will bring us true happiness. Let's choose to step FORWARD towards happiness instead.

With this next cornerstone, **Freedom**, we're going to look at how *"reclaiming your life agenda"* is the most freeing decision you can make; we'll talk about how only YOU can define wealth and success. We'll look at why success doesn't equal happiness and explore the ways in which money can buy it. We'll learn how you can take back control from your fears and, finally, how the truth about renting versus owning can set you free.

Let's roll!

6

How To Get Wealthier Without
Working Harder

I HAD FINALLY made it.

The big leagues. *Bridgemill.*

What is Bridgemill, you ask? It's a highly sought after golf neighborhood in Canton, Georgia (the northwest suburbs of Atlanta). In my eyes, if you wanted to let the world know that you had made it, saying you lived in Bridgemill was the way to do it.

But I couldn't be in one of the small, cookie-cutter homes that some people bought just to say they lived in Bridgemill. I had to buy a five-bedroom, four-bath, monster home with a country-club-like private pool in my backyard, all while sitting on the fourteenth tee box of the golf course.

Yep, I had decided that my single, 28-year old self needed a 4,000+ square foot, two-car garage (for both of my cars) home on the golf course. I had made it, and I was about to let the world know about it!

Of course, what they don't tell the single guy buying a 4,000+ square foot home with a fully decked out basement, pool, and a big yard is how much money it takes to furnish and take care of the place properly. I couldn't have my well-to-do neighbors over to sit on couches left over from my college days. I spent at least $30,000 on new bed sets for the spare rooms, patio furniture, new sofas and end tables, and much more. This whole "letting the world know I had made it" venture was getting expensive!

Then there was the work that went into cleaning the house, manicuring the yard and flowers in accordance with HOA rules, cleaning the pool, and other miscellaneous big bills that tend to run side by side with big homes. For instance, I couldn't live in a golf neighborhood without having access to the golf course, the monster community pool, or the workout center. Thousands more down the tube.

Then there was the mountain chalet that I shared with my best friend, Doug. And the three-bedroom rental home in Woodstock, Georgia. Oh, and the lake property that I split with a family friend named Squire.

I tell you all of this not to brag, but to make sure you know just how "LARGE" I was living. Thinking back on it now, I realize how silly I looked living in such a huge home by myself just so I could "fool" the world into thinking I was rich and happy. I am sure many of my friends could see right through it, and they probably enjoyed debates behind my back on why I was buying so much stuff. If they knew what I knew, the answer was pretty simple: I was fishing for happiness and not catching a thing.

As I would learn over the course of several years and a lot of soul-searching, I had no idea what true wealth really was. I was too focused on what I thought it looked like. I was stuck in a quicksand trap called "Keeping up with the Joneses."

Comparing yourself, your home, your car, your clothes, and your toys to that of your neighbors, co-workers, and friends has been going on for... well, forever. The phrase "Keeping up with the Joneses" was popularized in America by newspaper cartoonist Arthur "Pop" Momand way back in 1913. The stresses that come with worrying about how others perceive us, or "status anxiety" as author and philosopher **Alain de Botton** calls it, is not a new phenomenon.

The "Keeping up" idea is that if you see your neighbor with a new car, then you start wanting a new car too. If you see your neighbor get a new swimming pool in the backyard, then by all means, you need a new swimming pool in your backyard. If your neighbor sells his house and moves to a house twice the size and leaves you behind, then you start dwelling over selling your house and upgrading too. I think you get the point.

Well, here is what "the Joneses" don't tell you:

A vast majority of the neighbors upgrading their stuff don't have the means to do so either. Meaning, they are already living well above their means, but they just had to "supersize" something in their life because they didn't want *their* friends to think they weren't as successful and wealthy. The Joneses are trying to "keep up with the Joneses" too.

Before you know it, too many people are trying to outdo each other and living at or above their maximum means, and it becomes a vicious (and detrimental) cycle. That is how you can get whole neighborhoods all living at or above their means in a short period. In most cases, the majority of this community is stressed out, leveraged in debt up to their necks, and so busy working to pay for it all that they hardly get to enjoy it.

Haven't you ever met a guy that buys a tricked-out boat only to see it sit in a slip or his driveway because he is working more hours than ever to pay for the darn thing? Now he not only has the new payment and fees stressing him out and making him work harder, but he is also giving up family time just to break even with where he used to be. That doesn't exactly sound like "the good life," does it?

The real trouble in these communities happens when a slowdown or a recession hits. It's what we saw in 2008 when entire neighborhoods were walking away from homes with foreclosure and short sale signs in the yard. Then there are the consequences that can't be measured in dollar signs. I'm talking about the impact that "keeping up with the Joneses" can have on relationships and families, as one spouse (or both) sacrifices freedom and control for status markers. It's something I've seen happen up close and personal.

After working his tail off sixty hours per week for his company, my friend—let's call him John—landed a big promotion that took him from making $74,000 all the way to $130,000. The only downside was that the new job was going to require a lot of travel. He knew that promotions like this don't happen every day, so John and his wife (I'll call her Jane) agreed that, because the money was worth it, the two of them along with their two young children would sacrifice to make it work.

As the couple began to see their bank account quickly grow (his new paychecks were almost double what they used to be), it wasn't long before they wanted to buy a new home. You see, one of their best friends had also received a promotion earlier in the year, and in the process had purchased a new home and a new car. So of course, it made sense for them to do so as well. Plus, with John out of town almost every Monday through Thursday on business travel, Jane was getting bored and lonely. She firmly believed a new (and much larger) home would add some excitement to her life.

Once in the new house, Jane found herself alone nearly every night, eating a quiet dinner with the kids, wondering if she would hear from her husband. Most of John's evenings were spent entertaining clients and prospects, and many nights he wouldn't get back to his hotel room until eleven pm.

His relationship with his kids consisted of a Facetime call once or twice per week when he had time. And although he had big plans to spend time with them on the weekends, when he came home from his long week, John was so burnt out and tired from traveling that he spent most weekends napping and getting his energy back.

John and Jane's relationship began to unravel as well. They rarely spoke during the week except for a few texts each day. On the weekends, she was busy busing the kids around to birthday parties and soccer games while he slept in late. While Jane wanted to get a babysitter, go out on dinner dates, and have some alone time with John when he was home, he was so tired of eating out and drinking wine that he preferred to stay in, cook dinner, and catch up on all of his emails.

Neither of them were happy.

After some arguments, they both decided that the answer might be to get more "stuff"—you know, to enjoy the spoils of his work a bit more. It seemed easier than a divorce. Jane was tired of her minivan and wanted a luxury SUV. John had always wanted a boat. So a month later they were the proud owners of a new 24-foot center console boat and a brand new Lexus.

These toys made them both happy for a few weeks. She loved going around showing off her new Lexus, and the boat had given him new life and new energy to go hit the lake. For three weeks in a row, John and Jane took their family and friends out on the boat for a fun-filled day on the water. Life was good again.

But by the fourth week, John caught a nasty bug during one of his many flights and was forced to spend the weekend recovering in bed. By the time he came home the fifth week, they were back to arguing like usual. It was as if the last three weeks of bliss had never happened.

John and Jane had their large new home, a new Lexus SUV for her, and a new boat for him. Their kids were healthy and in good schools. Yet they were miserable. They had no time for each other and no time to enjoy life. They began to wish things could just go back to the way they were when he was making $75k per year and had more time around the house.

But how could they do that now? There was the new (hefty) mortgage to pay for, the new car, and the boat. They couldn't cover those costs with his old salary. Besides, what would people say if they did that? Wouldn't John look like a failure if he went back to his old job? Wouldn't the neighbors think they were financially struggling if they sold the boat? And surely his boss would be unimpressed if John told him he wanted to cut back on the travel. No, the reasons to stay seemed to outweigh the reasons to go.

What happens in this story? You probably already know. John worked his tail off to hit another promotion that he believed would give him more money to buy freedom and happiness for his family. They continued to spend more, hoping the new toys will bring about the "fix" they needed. But the happiness mirage kept moving farther out with each purchase.

I wish I could tell you that they had a big watershed moment and realized that all the money in the world wouldn't give them as much fulfillment as being able to spend time together and do the things that truly made them happy. That isn't what happened for Jane and John, though. Their marriage ended in divorce. The last time I heard about him, he was still working and spending more money than he has in his bank account trying to keep what's left of his life.

Pretty sad ending, huh? The lesson here is simple:

True wealth is *freedom* and *control* over your life's choices. Don't hand it over for *stuff* or *status*.

By locking themselves into a new mortgage, car payments, a boat, and all those other fancy things, John and Jane gave up freedom and control of other areas of their life. When they wanted to make a change, they couldn't (or at least *believed* they couldn't). That big fancy house limited John's job options; they didn't have the financial freedom to look at other salary ranges. In trying to "keep up with the Joneses" John and Jane kept spending and digging themselves into a deeper hole. Their desire to be seen as wealthy was the controlling force. And it cost them. Big time. They looked wealthy to anyone who saw them, but they sacrificed real wealth to do so. As **Warren Buffet** famously said, *"It's only when the tide goes out that you learn who has been swimming naked."*

The hardest part about John and Jane's story? It's SO easy to see how I could make those same decisions. Keeping up with the Joneses feels normal! Chasing after money is taught as a virtue! There are so many books and seminars and online courses that follow some variation of the same theme Wallace Wattles espoused in **The Science Of Getting Rich**:

> *"The fact remains that is it not possible to live a really complete or successful life unless one is rich. No man can rise to this greatest possible height in talent or soul development unless he has plenty of money."*

What those books fail to tell their readers is the very lesson my friend John is learning the hardest way possible. The "normal" view of wealth comes at a high cost.

While reading through the "tank of a book" (over 670 pages) called **Tools Of Titans,** by Tim Ferriss, I came across one of the best reminders that material things can't buy you happiness. When Tim asked entrepreneur and CD Baby founder Derek Sivers *"what would he put on a billboard?"* Derek responded with this amazing reply:

"I think I would make a billboard that says, 'It Won't Make You Happy,' and I would place it outside any big shopping mall or car dealer. You know what would be a fun project, actually? To buy and train thousands of parrots to say, 'It won't make you happy!' and then let them loose in the shopping malls and superstores around the world. That's my life mission. Anybody in? Anybody with me? Let's do it."

The Millionaire Fastlane by MJ DeMarco offers up some over the top (and in many cases cruel) perspectives, but he speaks the truth about money. Here's what he has to say about those "normal" views:

"Normal is to slave at a job Monday through Friday, save 10%, and repeat for 50 years. Normal is to buy everything on credit. Normal is to believe the illusion that the stock market will make you rich. Normal is to believe that a faster car and a bigger house will make you happy. You're conditioned to accept normal based on society's already corrupted definition of wealth, and because of it, normal itself is corrupted. Normal is modern-day slavery."

Wow. Talk about a sobering message. Call it an "aha moment" if you want, but the big realization for me here was that I was approaching wealth all wrong. In fact, I wasn't even working with the right definition.

WEALTH IS SELF-DETERMINED

Chances are you're already pretty wealthy. The only question is whether you recognize it or not. And the answer comes down to what you're counting.

Do you measure your wealth in dollar signs? Or do you measure it in terms of your happiness, fulfillment, and freedom?

Take a cue from Og Mandino, author of **The Greatest Salesman In The World**, who said:

"No, my son, do not aspire for wealth and labor not only to be rich. Strive instead for happiness, to be loved and to love, and most important to acquire peace of mind and serenity."

Or listen to MJ Demarco when he tells you that, *"Wealth is not authored by material possessions, money, or "stuff", but by what I call the three fundamental "F's": family (relationships), fitness (health), and freedom (choice). Within this wealth trinity is where you will find true wealth, and yes, happiness."*

I argue that when you decide to measure wealth according to your four cornerstone pieces—through your mission, values, core desires, relationships, freedom, and control over your life's direction—then you will be better equipped not only to enjoy your wealth but also to GROW it.

SO HOW DO YOU GET WEALTHIER WITHOUT WORKING HARDER?

Thomas J. Stanley had two amazing quotes in his book, **The Millionaire Next Door** that I hope you will write down and never forget:

"Whatever your income, always live below your means."

And:

"Money should never change one's values… Making money is only a report card. It's a way to tell how you are doing."

These two important pieces of advice offer a clear roadmap for how to approach money and wealth.

The first is simple: don't overspend or lock yourself into purchases that you can't afford or that will keep you treading water. The minute you put pen to paper on that big-ticket item, you are signing away a percentage of your freedom and control. Always be cognizant of that tradeoff. Conversely, when you live below your means—say, by sticking with that house you've nearly got paid off—you keep that money (and the time and effort it takes to earn it) available for other things. Better still, the longer you keep that house and its lower payments and the more money you save, the more financial freedom you will have.

(Fun fact: Despite being one of the richest people in the world, Warren Buffett has lived in the same house in Omaha, Nebraska, since he bought it in 1957!)

Stanley's second piece of advice is, I think, the best way to view the number in your bank account. If you think of your money as a report card instead of a goal, it can reset your whole approach to wealth. You'll see money as a *tool* for supporting the things that truly make you feel happy and fulfilled. The amount of money coming in and going out each month or year is an excellent way to measure your progress toward goals that matter.

If you're struggling with this idea of redefining your wealth, there's another big question you ought to ask yourself: **Why don't I feel like I have enough?**

As T. Harv Eker points out in ***Secrets Of The Millionaire Mind***, not having enough money is usually a symptom of not having clearly defined goals and purposes for that money.

"A lack of money is merely a symptom of what is going on underneath. Lack of money is the effect, but what is the root cause? It boils down to this. The only way to change your outer world is to first change your inner world. Whatever results you're getting, be they rich or poor, good or bad, positive or negative, always remember that your outer world is simply a reflection of your inner world. If things aren't going well in your outer life, it's because things aren't going well in your inner life. It's that simple."

In other words, if you have no internal mission, your outer world will most likely be out of whack.

In ***How To Get What You Want And Want What You Have***, John Gray shares an observation that I think really drives this point home, *"Most of us mistakenly believe that having more will make us happy and take away our pain. Unfortunately, each time we look to outer success for fulfillment, we feel more empty inside."* Keeping up with Joneses or, heck, even making them want to keep up with you will not make you feel fulfilled. Seeing six, seven, or eight-figure sums in your bank account will not make you feel fulfilled. Driving around in a slick sports car will not make you feel fulfilled—even if it is super-fun.

To be totally honest with you, the idea of shifting focus from the number of zeros in my balance was a tough change for me to make. I was pretty attached to my expensive toys and what I was signaling by owning them—plus the idea of not making as much money as humanly possible sounded nuts!

But what ultimately brought me around was seeing the money I earned as something *purposeful*. I realized that if I couldn't connect my money to my mission and purpose in life, no amount would ever satisfy me. It was Elker's "Law of Income" in ***Secrets Of The Millionaire Mind*** that finally got through to me: *"The key word is value."*

The minute you start trying to make money just for the sake of making money—or, as the expression goes, *"Using money you haven't earned to buy things you don't need to impress people you don't like"*—is when you (and most people, including myself) start to become miserable. When you use your money to directly support the things that you really value, instead of funneling it into trying to impress strangers, you'll feel what it truly means to be rich.

So ditch your attachment to superficial things. Dan Millman nailed it with this quote in his book, ***Way Of The Peaceful Warrior:*** *"The secret of* *happiness, you see, is not found in seeking more, but in developing the capacity to enjoy less.*" Fancy things and the envy of your neighbors might feel good in the short term, but real wealth is being able to prioritize the things that truly make you happy.

Live within your means, never lose focus on what makes you feel ful-filled, and seek out ways to capitalize on what you are best at. Focus on how you can create value instead of how you can pad your bank account. Stop comparing yourself to your neighbors, friends, and co-workers so much. Take Deepak Chopra's advice from ***The Happiness Prescription*** and "*notice how much effort you are spending to impress people who will then turn around and try to impress someone else*" and realize that "*the cycle never ends because it's based on mutual insecurity.*" Choose not to play that game.

Change the systems with which you measure your wealth and suc-cess. Stop using status markers as your yardstick and start using your four cornerstone pieces. View your money as a report card instead of a goal. Put your focus on the things that bring value to your life and the lives of others. Most importantly, see your purpose in your success; stick to your mission. ***Alan Wallace*** said, "*If you bank on achieving genuine happiness and fulfillment by finding the perfect mate, getting a great car, having a big house, the best insurance, a fine reputation, and the top job—if these are your focus, wish also for good luck in life's lottery.*" And he's right. But when you define wealth and success for yourself, you take luck out of the equation. You make wealth and success a choice.

Finally, if you MUST compare yourself to someone, do as ***Zig Ziglar*** suggests and measure your progress against who you were last year, or five years ago, or ten years ago. As he says, "*True success isn't measured by comparing yourself to your neighbor. It's by comparing what you are doing and accomplishing compared to what God gave you.*" Pa-POW!

7

When Money *Can* Buy Happiness

You MIGHT BE reading the title of this chapter and thinking, "Wait a second, Joe. Didn't we just talk about how wealth is self-determined? Weren't you just telling me not to be so focused on the numbers in my bank account?" And to that, I have to say, "Yep!" In the last chapter, we discussed the idea of seeing money as a TOOL instead of a goal. Thomas J. Stanley referred to it as a "report card" in ***The Millionaire Next Door.*** We're going to dig into that idea further in this chapter and take a look at how using money as a tool in our toolbox *can* make us happier.

Before we dive in, however, I want to tell you a story.

It was just another afternoon for my brother and I in our backyard. I was nine, and Luke was seven. My dad worked pretty long hours during the week, so after school my mom was in charge. Since she had her hands pretty full with our youngest brother, Daniel, Mom had one rule for us: "If it's not raining and it's not dinnertime, then you boys better be outside. And stay out of trouble."

We had one TV in the house (an old Zenith tube TV that weighed a ton and was as deep as it was wide and tall). It had twelve channels (of which half would only work if you moved the bunny ears the right way), and it was only allowed to be on if it was raining. The thought of that old TV (and how much a 24-inch TV weighed back then) still makes me laugh.

So what did we do instead of TV? Luke and I would head out into the yard, climb the two trees out back, play in the fort my dad built for us, and then we would always make our way to walk The White Wall.

What was "The White Wall"?

To us kids, it was more famous than the Great Wall of China (and certainly longer). It seemed to go on for miles and miles, and walking it from one end to the other would take an eternity. It was tall, too. A fall from the top guaranteed a scuffed knee and a cut-up hand (if you broke your fall), or getting the air knocked out of you if you didn't.

Inside the wall was what every kid in the neighborhood wanted to see. On a lot that could have been turned into fifty homes or more, there was a mansion and two barns that appeared bigger than our house.

From the road you could see the top half of the fenced in private tennis court, and from the lake you could see just how massive the home was. I was fascinated by it. I would sit on the wall under the shade of one of the big oak trees during the hot Florida summer and daydream about living in a mansion like that one. Certainly, it must have trap doors and an elevator. It probably even had butlers. It was around that time that I became dead set on being rich and living in a home like this someday.

If you recall from my "Bridgemill home" story, you know how the rest of my infatuation with having a huge house unfolded. Without my four cornerstone pieces in place yet, my only driving force was making more money, and I ended up alone and very unfulfilled in that big house of mine. Back then if someone would ask me why I was so laser-focused on my net worth, my only response was, "Because being rich sounds a lot better than being poor." It may have been true, but I was missing the point.

It has been said that money is the root of all evil. That every Ponzi scheme, every bank robbery, every dirty money plot, every corporate scandal (think Enron), and even most wars stemmed from greed and the hunger for more money. Sadly, even most divorces today cite money as one of the main sources of their unhappiness.

Now, am I saying that having loads of money or a big house (or mansion) is bad, or that it means you can't be happy and fulfilled? Of course not! If a big house fits in with your four cornerstone pieces, if it fits in with your purpose in life, and if you can afford it, then, by all means, live in a big house!

Heck, I plan on living in a big home one day and living a life of happiness and fulfillment! Of course, this time I'll be going about things in a different way than I did when I snapped up my home in Bridgemill. I will be moving forward with a focused mission and purpose in life, giving back more than I take, all while having my focus set on happiness, compassion, and fulfillment instead of money.

MONEY ALONE CAN'T BUY HAPPINESS. BUT MONEY COMBINED WITH PURPOSE CAN.

With the right purpose and "end goal" in place, money can certainly help buy happiness. Matthieu Ricard illustrates this point in *Happiness* when he tells a story about his friend from Hong Kong that promised himself that he was going to work his tail off until he saved a million dollars, and then he would quit work and finally enjoy life. Ten years later his friend had blown past his goal and had three million dollars in the bank. When Ricard asked him about his happiness and how he was enjoying life now that he hit his goal of being a millionaire, the friend replied, "*I wasted ten years of my life.*"

Money can help you in personal ways such as buying better food, better social engagements, better vacations, and better living arrangements. But if you don't use it as a tool for your mission, purpose, or any other piece of your four cornerstones, it can eventually leave you feeling empty inside.

Take Lotto winners as an example. We all have heard the stats that over 70% of all lottery winners go broke. Not only do they lose what they won, but most of them end up with less than they had before hitting the jackpot. To make matters worse, many lottery winners become depressed and less happy than when they weren't rich. How is that possible?

It's because at least 7 out of 10 lottery winners did not have any foundation in place. They had no purpose in mind for the money and little to no endgame in sight. Without question, every single new lottery winner tells themselves and their family they won't be one of the bad statistics, yet the 7 out of 10 number has been consistent for decades. If your only goal is to have more money just to have more money, then, as we have discussed, getting a big lump sum of it won't bring you fulfillment. You've got to have a purpose and a mission for it.

Not a single book that I read says that money alone can buy you happiness (at least not long-term happiness). I'd argue that the stats on those unhappy Lotto winners drive that point home. But many of the books made mention of the fact that money can help achieve long-term fulfillment when it is applied towards a mission or in service of others.

In Mel Abraham's book, ***The Entrepreneur's Solution***, Gary Erickson (founder of Clif Bar who came close to dying in a bad bike accident) had this to say:

> *"The material things we have are not a symbol of success… lying in the ambulance (after a horrific bike accident), I certainly wasn't thinking, "I wish I had stuffed more dollars in my pocket." What kept going through my head was, "How could I have done more? Did I really have a positive impact?" In the end, that will be what matters."*

Robert Ringer would likely agree. He had this to say in **Winning Through Intimidation**: *"Given that your time on earth is limited, it makes good sense to aim high and move fast. When my participation in the game of life ends, I don't want to be caught begging for one more chance to grab the brass ring. The fact is that I've never known a person who was given an extra inning."*

Spending tons of money on empty things is probably not what Ringer's referring to when he says, "aim high and move fast." What counts, in the end, is the work you did and the progress you made toward your mission. Your money and anything else you use to achieve your aims is just a *tool* in your toolkit.

Another important thing to keep in mind is not to let the pursuit of money blind you to your real purpose. It breaks my heart hearing about recent college grads that feel called to be a teacher or to work in the public sector but choose not to because the salary would be too low. Money can be a tool for happiness, but NOT if it holds you back from fulfilling your mission.

Choose instead to live like Marva Collins, a teacher in Chicago who Tal Ben-Sharar describes in his book, **Happier**: *"Teaching gave her life meaning that she believed no other profession could give her; teaching gave her the emotional gratification that no amount of money could buy. She felt that she was 'the wealthiest woman in the world' and that her experiences as a teacher were worth more to her than 'all of the gold in Fort Knox' because happiness, not gold or prestige, is the ultimate currency."*

Marva Collins has determined what wealth really means to her and sees herself as "the wealthiest woman in the world"! She is happy and fulfilled because she is living in agreement with her mission. She's not a millionaire but her money AND the method in which she earns it have a purpose.

HOW MUCH IS "ENOUGH"?

Let's face it. We must have money to live. I would even argue that money is second only to air in the list of things we must have to stay alive long-term. Yes, people have made it through life happy with hardly any money (like living on five dollars per day as a Buddhist monk up in the mountains), but some money is still required to stay alive in the modern age. You can only do so much bartering, borrowing, living off the land, or stealing before it runs dry. And that's not to mention all of the stress and difficulty that can come from living in real scarcity.

Poverty is a huge and very real problem—one whose solution goes WAY beyond the scope of this book—but that's not what I'm here to talk about. The money problem I want to address here is knowing what to do with it when you have a lot of it, recognizing when you have enough, and how to avoid becoming "money blind."

Did you know that in a recent CNBC poll 44% of polled millionaires described themselves as middle class? And only 4% of all the millionaire and multi-millionaires (these were millionaires not including their residence) felt they were wealthy! Four percent!!![1]

Similarly, when they polled people with at least $5 million or more in assets (the wealthiest 1–5% of all Americans), an astonishing 23% defined themselves as middle class, and 49% described themselves as upper middle class. In other words, they felt they weren't that wealthy because there was always someone wealthier than them.

A similar report from UBS found that 52% of millionaires said they "were stuck on a treadmill, but can't get off without giving up their family's lifestyle." They went on to say, "the more they have, the more they want." But the craziest part of the survey was how they saw themselves when

---

1 http://www.cnbc.com/2015/05/06/naires-say-theyre-middle-class.html

asked how much wealth each of them were aspiring to have before they would officially be happy.

Those in the $1 million to $5 million range said they needed $5 million to $10 million to be comfortable and content. Likewise, the current millionaires with $5 million to $10 million in the bank said they needed at least $10 million or $15 million to be comfortable. Those with assets slightly over $10 million said they needed $25 million in the bank to be comfortable and less stressed (to be able to get off the never-ending treadmill).[2] In other words, almost all of the millionaires they surveyed said they needed DOUBLE what they have now to be comfortable and happy.

The final piece that the survey uncovered was incredibly valuable for anyone striving to be wealthy. These millionaires and multimillionaires said they valued family above everything else, and that they wanted so much wealth and money to help improve their family's lives. However, they also admitted that most of them sacrificed way too much time away from family to make their wealth. And can you guess what they said their biggest regret was? All of their regrets were related to mistakes they made with spouses and family members (from not being around enough, to lavish spending, to having spoiled kids with terrible attitudes).

Personally, these numbers along with what those millionaires had to say about their lives flabbergasted me. But I'm also aware that someone else could likely think the same thing about me. And that brings us to the answer of that big question: "How much is enough?"

The answer is whatever you say it is... AFTER you've identified and built out your four cornerstones. Do the work to determine your mission, purpose, and core values. Take steps to define what true wealth means to

---

2   http://www.cnbc.com/2015/05/04/millionaires-feel-stuck-on-a-treadmill-survey.html

you. Choose freedom and control over a slightly higher bank statement. Don't be controlled by things that go *beep* in the night. Decide how much money you need to achieve these things—that is "enough."

See, the rest as icing on the cake.

SO HOW CAN MONEY BUY HAPPINESS?

Having control plays a big part in being happy. And the last time I checked, money can certainly improve how much control you have. Money can also buy more freedom; freedom from credit card debt, home debt, and stacks of bills. Even work stress can go down with the freedom that comes from having enough money.

Here is a great list of ways that money can indeed buy happiness from that back of Gretchen Rubin's book, ***The Happiness Project***:

Money can help end marital conflict.
Money can give you more Security.
Money can strengthen social bonds (you can host parties, events, and do more things with others).
Money can get you access to better exercise opportunities (nicer gyms, personal trainers, etc.).
Money can help you afford healthier food.
Money can enable you to spend it on other people.
Money can enable you to give back to those in need.

MJ DeMarco has his own list in ***The Millionaire Fastlane***:

"Money buys the freedom to watch your kids grow up.
"Money buys the freedom to pursue your craziest dreams.
"Money buys the freedom to make a difference in the world.
"Money buys the freedom to build and strengthen relationships.

"Money buys the freedom to do what you love, with financial validation removed from the equation."

The ability to use your money for happiness lies in having a proper foundation in place. It is in knowing your goals, being able to use your money wisely, being able to know when you have enough money, being able to be generous with your money, and being able to use it for long-term fulfillment and **not** short-term instant gratification.

I'd like to add that giving back is a HUGE part of using money as a tool for happiness. One important concept that all wealthy people agreed on was the importance of giving. When you accumulate a large amount of wealth (or have it gifted to you), it will all be gone as quick as it came in if you don't give back. This same concept was found in the autobiographies of ***John Rockefeller***, ***Walt Disney***, ***Phil Knight*** (founder of Nike), ***P.T. Barnum*** (one of the richest men in America in the early 1900s), and ***Rich Devos*** (founder of Amway).

P.T. Barnum captured the sentiment in ***The Art of Getting Money*** when he said: *"Of course men should be charitable, because it is a duty and a pleasure. But even as a matter of policy, if you possess no higher incentive, you will find that the liberal man will command patronage, while the sordid, uncharitable miser will be avoided."* In other words, there are a lot of internally fulfilling benefits that come with giving back. Or, to simplify it even further, Ebenezer Scrooge was much happier once he started using his wealth as a tool to create happiness for others.

And that makes sense, right? After all, you can't take that money with you when you die.

Which brings us to the final and by far the most important thing: keep the end in mind. Recall that Apple founder ***Steve Jobs*** said that there are no rewards for being the richest guy in the cemetery. I couldn't agree more. Know the end game and don't let money steer you off course. If you live life with a purpose and mission, the money will follow and show up when it's supposed to. Use your money as a tool for your four cornerstones, and it *can* buy happiness.

8

The Truth About Renting vs. Owning Can Set You Free

I was trying to stop the tears from coming down my face, but I couldn't. After drying off my face with the sleeve of my right arm (hoping that no one noticed), I glanced over at my wife and saw she was crying too. Little did we know when we woke up that morning that our lives, dreams, and plans were about to be completely altered over the course of 30 minutes.

We had been living back in Georgia for barely over a year when it happened. My wife had finished up her residency program at the University of Texas and had joined an ophthalmology practice in Lawrenceville. I was running a national financial marketing company. Life was running pretty smoothly, but Loren and I agreed that we felt like we were missing something. So we made the decision to go back to church.

Truth be told, we hadn't been to church in over four years. Given our schedules—Loren either worked every Sunday during residency or she caught up on sleep from working ungodly hours throughout the week—or just our complacency, attending service was a habit that we had long forgotten. We decided to try a church that was less than a mile from our house called Twelve Stone. We honestly didn't know much about it, and the choice was made solely because it was so close and we hated Atlanta traffic.

The first service we attended at Twelve Stone was really good. We didn't meet any new friends, but we felt like it was a place we could continue to come back to. On and off we attended Twelve Stone, and each sermon was getting better than the next. It was no shock that this place was attracting thousands of people throughout their multiple campuses in Gwinnett County. They even had an over-the-top awesome nursery program for our young daughter Shauna.

But even though we loved the church and we had some great friends close by, we still felt like something was missing in our lives. Loren was starting to doubt the "business of medicine" and how dysfunctional and non-patient friendly it had become. I was borderline miserable running my company and I had finally come to the realization that I was a horrible manager (most entrepreneurs do not make good day-to-day managers of people). Moreover, I knew with certainty that I did not want to keep doing what I was doing for the rest of my life. We had become closer to God over the last few months, but we still didn't feel fulfilled. Would having another child help? We weren't sure, but we were willing to try.

Then one day it happened (which brings me back to why my wife and I were crying). Pastor Kevin Myers was speaking on both happiness and fear that day; how it's impossible for the two to coexist and the way fear holds us back from the things that make us happy. The sermon hit Loren and I like a train running over a penny on the track. It slammed us, it stretched us, and it reshaped us as it pushed us to tears. And we never even saw it coming.

To prove his point, Pastor Kevin asked everyone in the audience (hundreds of people) to raise their hand if they didn't love their job. As you can imagine, at least half of the hands in the room went up.

Then he asked people to not raise their hands for the next few questions (to protect them from potential awkwardness while sitting next to their spouse or significant other). Pastor Kevin went on to say that he was 100% certain that a big chunk of the room were in bad relationships, from marriages where the love had been lost to adultery, all the way to verbally and physically abusive relationships.

He went on to say that he knew from talking with the people in the congregation that many of them didn't love where they lived. They didn't like the school that their children were attending. They wished they could be somewhere else.

Then he posed a huge set of questions to us: *Why are you still in that job? Why are you staying in an area you don't love? Why are you still with that boyfriend, girlfriend, or spouse that you don't love? Why won't you leave someone who is hurting you? Why are you participating in anything that doesn't make you happy?*

IT'S BECAUSE OF FEAR.

It's the fear that you might not find a better job. It's the fear that you might not find the right house or that your kids might have to make new friends. It's the fear that things might not go exactly as planned, that you might lose some money in the process, or that you might be alone.

Pastor Kevin then paused for a few seconds before saying, *"You're afraid of what you might lose. You're scared of what making these changes might cost you. And while I understand where this fear comes from, believe me when I tell you that you have nothing to lose. How can you? You do not OWN anything. You do not own your house. You do not own your 401k. You do not own your bank accounts. You do not own your car. You do not own all of your toys. And you do not own your time here on Earth. It can all be taken away from you at any minute."*

He paused and then said, *"Everything you think you own is RENTED from God. Your money, your home, your clothes, your cars, your bank accounts, your Skymiles, your kids, and especially your TIME… they are all rented. You own nothing. God owns it all and is gracious enough to let us all rent what he has created."*

Wow. Pastor Kevin's message changed my whole perspective in an instant.

Regardless of whether you believe in a higher power, do you think you exist to work in a job you hate? Do you believe your life was given to you with the intention that you would spend it with someone you don't like? Do you think any God enjoys seeing his creation wasting away in misery, trying to protect and desperately hold on to what they are "renting" from him, all to avoid the fear of change?

The **Bible** says, *"What do you have that God hasn't given you? And if all you have is from God, why boast as though you have accomplished something on your own?"* It's a powerful way to look at it, don't you think?

So knowing that, why do we get so caught up in the fear of losing something we don't own? Why do we fear change when it can be brought down upon us at any time? And why do we avoid difficult choices when we know deep down that they bring growth? How much longer will you allow fear to hold you back? Isn't it time to make the most of the time you have?

As all of this was hitting me while sitting in Twelve Stone Church that day, I knew Loren and I needed a change of scenery. Not so much in our relationship, but in our jobs and where we lived. Our relationship needed a little more spunk as well, but I knew for certain that where we were living and what we were doing for our jobs were the areas where we needed the most change. I didn't know where or what we were supposed to do next, but I knew we had nothing to gain by assuming our time was guaranteed.

YOU DON'T OWN ANYTHING.

You should never let fear or the sense of "ownership" get in the way of your purpose in life.

As **The Purpose Driven Life** states: *"We never really own anything during our brief stay on earth. God just loans the earth to us while we're here. It was God's property before you arrived, and God will loan it to someone else after you die. You just get to enjoy it for a while."*

I had numerous fears going through my mind after this memorable church service. Everything in my body was telling me to leave what I had built during my career of almost thirteen years, pack up the family and move to Florida to start something new. But Pastor Kevin's words had instilled a new sense of urgency into my thinking.

I realized I needed to stop making excuses in my life, and instead, make the changes necessary to find happiness and fulfillment in my life. And let me tell you, that shift in my thinking brought a lot of clarity.

Discerning what truly mattered (the happiness of my wife and kids, not being miserable at work every day) from what didn't (the predictability of my 'safe' career) suddenly became very easy. The difference between what was essential to me and what wasn't became very obvious. (Note: It was less than two months after this sermon that the "16-part Questionnaire" from cornerstone #1 attracted itself into my life and sealed the deal for our family moving to Florida and following our dreams).

One of my favorite books that impacted this new mindset of mine was **Essentialism** by Greg McKeown. It was all about discovering what is really important to you in life and letting go of what isn't. In the book, he proposes a quick but impactful exercise: *"Whatever decision or challenge or crossroads you face in life, simply ask yourself, "What is essential? Then eliminate everything else."*

I agree with this thinking but, truth be told, I found myself taking "Essentialism" and "Minimalism" a bit too far (and too fast) sometimes. If you cut out too much of your stuff, activities, or pleasures all at once, your mind and body find ways to fill that void back up quickly. So my advice is to start off "minimalizing" in small increments. A better suggestion is "everything in moderation."

In fact, I would modify this exercise by measuring a decision against your four cornerstone pieces rather than whether it is "essential." Ask yourself, "Is this essential to my overall mission and purpose in life?" I think this is a great way to slow your roll when it comes to decision-making—especially important decisions.

"Nothing in life is as important as you think it is, while you are thinking about it," said Daniel Kahneman in **Thinking Fast And Slow**. And I agree. It can be so easy to get caught up in our heads when faced with a big choice. We might even feel like we don't have control over these situations when we're stuck in the middle of them. I know I certainly felt that way when I was torn over whether I "could" leave my job and move my family.

And that's why Pastor Kevin's reminder that tomorrow is not promised to us was such wonderful news. Yes, you read that right.

THE PROMISE OF DEATH GIVES US FREEDOM AND CONTROL.

We are only renting our time on this planet from God. We have no control over when our lives will end. That's a pretty scary thought until you see all the freedom that truth gives you. What am I talking about?

You weren't in control of when you arrived in this life and you aren't in control of when you'll leave it. But EVERY MINUTE in between those two points is yours to do with as you see fit. You have complete freedom over how you live. You are in the driver's seat (should you *choose* to sit there). You are in complete control over the choices you make between your first breath and your last. But you have to be willing to take the wheel.

"If you don't decide what you want in life, you can't change your course to get it," Brendon Burchard reminds us in **Life's Golden Ticket**. *"No goals, no growth. No clarity, no change."* I believe making the most of the time God is renting to us means using our control and freedom to create lives that make us happy and fulfilled. Again, we weren't put here on Earth to be miserable! Nor were we put here to be stagnant or "stuck."

As Burchard also points out, *"In life, the path of least resistance is always silence. If you don't express your feelings and thoughts to others, you don't have to deal with their reactions to it. You don't have to feel vulnerable. You don't risk rejection. But I'll tell you what: the path of least resistance leads exactly where that ride leads to. He pointed again to the carts looping around the track. "Nowhere."*

I've learned that "the path of least resistance" is usually the one carved out by fear. The books I read have taught me that fear is the obstacle keeping me from making big changes. It's probably true for you, too. From moving jobs, from taking chances, identifying what you need to eliminate in your life—it is usually always **fear** that is holding you back.

Once you take action and get over the fear, you realize just how much the "comfortable things" in your life have been holding you back. When you choose to take a different path in accordance with your mission, you will be making the most of your rented or "gifted" time. As Deepak Chopra says in **The Seven Spiritual Laws of Success**, *"The past is history, the future is a mystery, and this moment is a gift. That is why this moment is called 'the present'."* Thinking about it in this way makes me smile. I hope it does the same for you.

The last idea that I want to leave you with is that there is one more gift that comes from recognizing that we're just renting our time from God. It's another kind of freedom and control, and it's very profound and powerful. Here it is:

When we accept the responsibility of taking control over our lives, choose to live according to our four cornerstones, and work to fulfill our mission and purpose; we free ourselves from the tragedy of death.

Rick Warren tells us in **The Purpose Driven Life** that, *"Knowing your purpose gives meaning to your life. The greatest tragedy is not death, but life without purpose."* When you dedicate your life to furthering your purpose, your life will be well-lived, happy, and fulfilling. You will not carry regrets or wonder what might have been. You will have created a legacy, whether in the things you create or the lives you impact, that will continue living long after you have left this Earth.

I bet you thought this chapter was going to be about renting versus owning real estate.

Fooled you!

Pa-POW!

9

Proven Steps To Take Control
Of Your Fears & Anxiety

I STARTED DRINKING beer on my driveway around one pm that day.

I cracked open the first can sitting there all alone, but that didn't matter to me. I had worked out that morning, done a little bit of schoolwork (I was at Georgia Tech at the time), and got ready for what would be a looooong night.

Even though it was October in Atlanta, I had my shirt off, my board shorts on, my 8 SPF oil/sunscreen applied, and I was ready to "tie one on" with a fun day of drinking followed by more drinking later that night. My best friend Doug joined me later that day, and so did our roommate Amy. My good friend and neighbor Chris came by for the afternoon, and a few others dropped by throughout the day to say hi and have a beer.

It was Friday, October 19th, 2001. My BIG Day. A day that changed my life forever.

And although I probably came close to dying that day, it didn't end with my funeral. It was my birthday. The impact this day had on my life is not something I've shared with anyone before. Not my wife. Not my parents. Not my kids. Not even my best friends who were there to witness what happened that night know the damage it has caused me long-term.

I feel that sharing this is something that I am being called to do, and frankly, it already feels like a fifteen-year-old burden I have been living with is coming off my chest. Because of that, I feel the need to tell the WHOLE story. Settle in, because this chapter is a long (and I hope) very helpful one. But back to the story at hand.

After drinking beer most of the day in and around the driveway at 1234 Francis Street in midtown Atlanta, Doug and I hit the phones to see where people were going out that night. Even though we had already polished off a case of Busch Light between the two of us that day (minus a few beers to friends that stopped by), we were young, had pretty well-trained livers from a few hard years of binge drinking, and thought we were invincible. Not to mention, it was my birthday!

We found out that my ATO friends (Doug and I were Sigma Chis) were heading to a dingy watering hole nearby that catered to college kids, so we rounded up the troops and hit the bar.

From what I recall, there were a lot of friends that came out that night to celebrate my birthday. A few of my Sigma Chi pledge brothers, some of my Pike friends, a handful of girls that I managed to convince to meet us out, and my roommates Doug and Amy.

And then things got crazy.

One of the ATO guys had one of those big, black, permanent markers that he frequently carried around on the weekends that served many purposes. Some nights it could be used to draw finger mustaches (when you draw a funny mustache on your pointer finger and then place the finger above your lip), some nights it was used to write down girls' phone numbers, and some nights it was used to count shots. Tonight, it was going to get a lot of use for that third reason.

By the time I had blacked out, I believe I had 14 black marks on my right arm. It's the last thing I remember from the night. I can still remember where I was sitting at the bar (I certainly couldn't stand at this point), and I recall time feeling like it was standing still. Everything was moving slower… my thoughts, my voice, my reflexes, and my brain.

The goal that night was for me to drink as many shots as my age… 23. The black permanent marker was getting a lot of work, but nothing compared to my body. Granted, many of the shots were not that strong like red snappers and lemon drops, but after a full day of drinking, my blood alcohol level must have been through the roof.

According to witnesses, I had to be carried out to Amy's car while trying to convince Doug and Amy I could sleep outside.

The next thing I remember is waking up on what used to a light blue Ralph Lauren comforter, completely covered in my vomit. I too, was pretty much covered from head to toe. I could smell the Jagermeister caked in my comforter, and I began to dry heave. Fortunately, I had puked up pretty much everything my body had to offer for the past nine hours.

Looking down at my right arm, I saw a bunch of black marks running up my forearm, and my mind slowly started to recall that they were marking my arm every time I took a shot the night before. I tried to count them, but my head was pounding so hard that I couldn't even concentrate enough to count. I felt like death.

As I slowly tried to get out of my bed without getting any more vomit on me, I peeked over the side to see that I had puked all over the floor as well. Great.

We lived in a three-bedroom house, and the one bathroom we all shared was on the complete opposite side of the house from my room. Not only did I have to relieve myself, but I desperately needed a shower to get all of the vomit off of my body and out of my hair. That smell, in combination with the strong stench of rotten liquor, was making me constantly dry heave.

I slowly opened the door to make my way to the bathroom (hoping to not see anyone), and Doug was right there on the couch. I later found out that he and Amy stayed up most of night checking on me, moving me around, and trying to jolt me while I was throwing up, all to make sure I didn't choke and die. They were incredibly worried about me, and they weren't sure if they should have taken me to the hospital or not.

While showering, I remember looking down at my forearm (after scrubbing some dried vomit from my arm) and counting the number of "shot marks." Fourteen. I had consumed fourteen shots after hours of binge drinking outside during the day.

Before this miserable day, I would have banged my chest and bragged to all of my friends about how many drinks I took down the night before. But now it was different. I had never experienced a hangover of this magnitude, and I wasn't sure whether to cry, vomit, or hang myself (all three options were going through my head at the time). I seriously considered going to the hospital to see if I had alcohol poisoning.

I spent the entire day on that couch, soaking it with sweat, trying to get as much water in my body as it would take, and avoiding talking to anybody that called to tell me happy birthday (this was before text messaging, back when people actually called). But I didn't want to speak or see anyone. I looked and felt like death was knocking at my door, and that probably wasn't too far from the truth in the past twenty-four hours.

Nightfall finally came, and I went to bed early still feeling ill, but hoping that I would be back to normal by tomorrow like all of my previous hangovers.

My stomach wasn't right for well over a week. I couldn't shake it. But the worst part was my lack of self-confidence while out in public, especially crowds. I couldn't wrap my head around it, but for the first time in my life, I couldn't stand being around people. My heart started beating faster when I was around crowds or in class. My stomach started churning, my palms would get sweaty, and my body temperature would rise. Sometimes I would start sweating, and my mind could not focus on anything else.

You can probably already guess what was happening to me. I was experiencing my first anxiety attack. Little did I know, these sudden panic attacks would stay with me and haunt me for the next fourteen years of my life. And it was all *triggered* from the crazy booze-fest I had on my twenty-third birthday.

FIGHT. FLIGHT.

It is said that when you have a panic or anxiety attack that your body goes into "fight or flight" mode just like it would if you were out in the wild and a grizzly bear was coming after you. And if you have ever experienced a panic attack firsthand, you know that your mind and body really do engage as though you're in danger. Your heart rate goes up, it becomes tougher to breathe, you start sweating, and you become weak and sometimes dizzy. You feel like you've got to go to the bathroom, you begin to get chest and stomach pains, and your body starts SCREAMING to your brain that you need to run away!!!

It is something I don't wish on anyone, yet I know it affects millions of people every year. In fact, it is estimated that one in four people will suffer from anxiety severe enough to be diagnosed as a disorder at some point in their life. The good news is that after fourteen years of letting panic attacks run my life, I finally found a way to conquer them once and for all that I will be sharing with you. But first, let me tell you about all of the mistakes I was making so you can learn from those and never repeat them. You will probably cringe when you see how I was trying to combat anxiety for the first ten-plus years after that fateful night.

MISTAKE NUMBER ONE: SELF-MEDICATING WITH UPPERS

When panic attacks hit, they would drain me of energy when I tried to keep them at bay with every ounce of energy I had. Not only do panic attacks make you feel weak and fatigued when they hit, but because your mind and body are working in overdrive in a "fight or flight" mode, they leave you mentally and physically exhausted as well.

After experiencing these panic attacks more frequently (still not really knowing what was happening to my body, and with too much pride to tell anyone), I started to look for ways to address the problem on my own.

Since I didn't have much energy, the first thing I tried was coffee. I had never been a coffee drinker before, but I was willing to do anything. But after a few mornings of trying to get down a full cup of disgusting black coffee (this was before Starbucks were on every corner), I knew there had to be a better way.

The next thing I tried were caffeine pills. Oh yeah, baby. These started to work right away. The quick bursts of energy helped big time, and I started to carry a small tube of caffeine pills around with me everywhere. To class, to work, to the bar. You name it; I was popping caffeine like it was candy.

Of course, the irony was that they were speeding up my heart rate, which was triggering more panic attacks. Since I still didn't know exactly what my body was doing, I had no idea that my daily doses of caffeine pills were causing the issue to get worse.

MISTAKE NUMBER TWO: SELF-MEDICATING WITH DOWNERS

The next thing that I did was try to suppress my body from these weird changes was to drink more alcohol. The alcohol actually seemed to help keep the panic attacks away for a while, so I continued to drink heavily during the evenings. Thankfully I didn't turn to alcohol in the middle of the day, and why would I? I had my trusty caffeine pills to make me feel better during the day.

However, one night it happened. I was feeling a little off before we were heading out, so I popped a few caffeine pills with my beer. On the ride to Buckhead, my heart started pounding, it was becoming tough to breathe, and I could feel myself starting to sweat. I rolled down the window to get some air and slowly began to feel a bit better.

Once in the bar, I ordered a beer hoping that was what I needed. But the beer only made it worse. I was getting hot again, and it felt like someone had turned up the heat to 110 degrees. So I ordered another beer, then another, then another. I couldn't stop sweating, my friend's were asking if I felt okay (which made it even worse), and I couldn't carry on a conversation to save my life. All I could think about was that I was dying. And I wanted to die that night. Something was seriously wrong.

So what did I do? I blamed it on the beer. Clearly, I needed to try hard liquor with some ice cubes. I figured the ice would make me feel cooler (since I was sweating so much), and told myself that I was probably allergic to something in the beer. I can't make this stuff up folks.

Over the next few months, I went through phases of only drinking vodka, then I switched to bourbon, and then I went to gin. None of them helped stop these weird feelings that my body was having. So then I turned to wine. I even had a stint with only buying champagne. Then it was back to different beers again. My roommates Doug, Travis, and Amy must have thought I was losing my mind.

MISTAKE NUMBER THREE: STAYING QUIET

I was caught in a vicious cycle of letting my fears consume my thoughts, which would leave me drained of energy, which would lead to caffeine pills, which would lead to more (and more severe) anxiety attacks. Repeat. No wonder I hardly had any energy back then (even though I was jolting my body full of caffeine). I'm lucky that I didn't have a heart attack.

I finally broke down one day and went to the student medical clinic on campus. I was too scared to tell anyone the truth yet, so all I told them was that I was constipated and having stomach issues. I conveniently failed to mention my sweating issues, my caffeine addiction, or my love affair with binge drinking.

After blood tests and stool samples, they found nothing wrong. They made a suggestion that I eat more fruits and vegetables and sent me on my way home with no resolution.

"That's just great," I thought myself as I was walking back home. All I wanted was a diagnosis and a pill to stop this. But of course, I was still too scared to tell anyone about what my body was doing. I was afraid people would think I was crazy, or that I was weird, or someone would tell me that I was dying. I had no idea that so many other people went through these "panic attacks" as young adults.

So why didn't I just tell someone? Or ask for help? Well, I was embarrassed and felt like people would judge me as a failure if I told them. To admit that I couldn't even control my body or mind was like admitting failure. I just couldn't do it. Part of me kept praying it would just go away.

However, the longer it went on, the more embarrassed I was, and the more I would try to hide it.

This went on for years, as I did my best to control what I could and hide what I couldn't. The final straw came when I missed my good friend's wedding because I couldn't bear the idea of being in a crowded church. After that, I decided I had to solve this problem. After years of dealing with these terrible feelings, it was time to find out what I was suffering from. I did not want to live like this anymore, and I was ready to put an end to it. It was controlling my life, and I had to find a solution.

An afternoon of Yahoo searches (this was still pre-Google), I finally discovered that I was suffering from anxiety attacks (also known as panic attacks or a social anxiety disorder). While reading about the symptoms and reading others' stories, it was like they were describing my life. I was kicking myself that it took me this long to find out what was wrong with me.

MISTAKE NUMBER FOUR: LOOKING FOR A "QUICK FIX"

Once I knew what I was suffering from, I spent hours and hours on the computer at night trying to find solutions. I still wasn't ready to tell a real person about my problems, so I bought an online course that claimed to cure anxiety attacks where I could remain anonymous. The course had a lot of fluff, and all I wanted was a quick fix! After going through it all, the solution was to practice breathing while listening to peaceful music. My mind wasn't buying it. I gave it a shot for about a week, and after seeing no results when I went out in public, I gave up to look for another solution.

Next, I tried meditation. But after sitting in my home trying to be silent, still, and keeping my mind free with little to no results, I wrote off meditation as something that hippies and monks did. After that, I read books, blogs, and I even jumped in a few forums to see if someone could share a quick fix with me.

Nothing worked, and no one seemed to have a legit solution to curing anxiety attacks. Looking back, the main problem was that I thought I could eliminate this anxiety overnight without ever having to face my fears. As you can imagine, I kept striking out.

MISTAKE NUMBER FIVE: THE EASY ROUTE

A few months passed, and I was still no closer to finding a solution. Then one afternoon at work, I had a panic attack while in a meeting. I had to excuse myself to the bathroom where I sat on the toilet and waited out the meeting to end. I couldn't take any more of this, so that afternoon I broke down and scheduled an appointment to see a doctor.

I firmly believed that this was finally going to be the answer I needed, but I also knew it was going to involve spilling the beans about my battle with anxiety after all of these years to some stranger in a white coat. As you can imagine, I was a nervous wreck the day I went in to see the doc. After telling the doctor my history with these anxiety attacks, he gave me exactly what I came in for... PILLS!

I got home from the pharmacy on cloud nine! I was finally going to be done with these panic attacks! Yes!!!

Long story short, the pills made me feel "off." I had lost some of my spunky energy, and I just wasn't myself. And when the panic attacks did come back, I felt like I was having an out of body experience. It was almost like my body stopped working, and I was in a dream watching it all from a few feet away. When one of the financial advisors that I called on mentioned that I sounded like I had no energy, I knew these pills were not for me.

Sadly, the doctor had given me exactly what I thought I wanted: the easy route. But after trying the pills for about two months, I realized that "easy" was not the answer I was looking for. I was back to where I started. My anxiety was back in charge.

While dealing with daily anxiety, I went on to meet the girl of my dreams, convinced her to marry me, convinced her not to get married in a church (we got hitched outside on the beach where I could blame any sweating on the humidity), and had two beautiful girls. I learned how to blog, how to write and make money, and avoided meetings and crowds by running my own business from home.

I continued to drink often, but my two daughters gave me the inspiration (and the fact they wake up so darn early and have zero sympathy or understanding for a hangover) to cut back drastically. I mentioned to my wife that I had experienced a panic attack before, but I never told her anything about my daily struggles with anxiety (as you can imagine, it was quite a shock for her to read it written here).

And then one day it happened. I found a proven system to beat anxiety, to end the panic attacks, and to *kick the crap out of fear*. It only took me fourteen years of suffering, but doggone it, the wait was worth it.

BREATHE.

We were about to go down to the Florida Keys for a week of freediving for lobster. If you have ever gone freediving, you know that the longer you can hold your breath, the longer you can stay underwater, which usually results in more lobster. Talk about incentive!

So I signed up for a course that guaranteed to safely get you down to 67 feet in one breath all in one weekend. My brother said that most people who take the course could double, if not triple their breath hold in a single weekend. Luke had already taken the course a year earlier, but he and our good friend Jon Bentley were going to come along with me to get a refresher. I was psyched!

However, the day before I was about to head down to South Florida from Tampa for my weekend freediving course, my wife Loren started feeling ill. By that night, she was almost unable to move and collapsed on the floor. She spent the next twenty-four hours in bed and didn't even have the energy to make it to the doctor.

I knew I couldn't leave her here with our two young girls, so I bailed out at the last minute and stayed at home to help my wife, missing my class and forfeiting the $380 I had already paid for it. As painful as that was, it was the right thing to do.

When Luke came back from his "refresher course," I asked him to explain to me how he learned to double his breath in a weekend. I wanted to start practicing what I could before our trip to the Keys in a couple of weeks.

Luke told me that the secret to a longer breath was to get your heart rate as slow as possible. The slower your heart rate, the more relaxed and calm you were, thus the longer you could hold your breath since your body is consuming less oxygen. He said the entire course was basically a day of safety and then a day of breathing exercises. But it was the breathing exercises that slowed your body into the most relaxed state possible.

He also went on to tell me that during the last few moments underwater before you finally come up for air, your body is going through some serious fight or flight feelings. In other words, your lack of oxygen is sending signals to your brain that you need to get to the surface via chest pain, lightheadedness, a rapid heart rate, trouble concentrating, and even blackouts. Sound familiar?

Luke went on to say that the trick to holding your breath longer was to get your body, breath, heart rate, and mind as far away from the panicked "fight or flight" state as possible. To do so, you must slow down your heart rate with strategic breathing right before you take the final big breath hold. And not just any breathing, it had to be breathing with your stomach, and not your chest. That part was critical he said. And the more relaxed and the slower your heart rate from your slow and rhythmic stomach breathing, the longer you can hold your breath. "Your mind also plays a role," he added, "in that you must **believe** you can hold your breath for a certain period of time."

As he was telling me all of this, I felt like I had just hit the jackpot. Here it was. The answer that I had been looking for was hand-delivered to me from a freediving course that I couldn't attend. Luke was explaining the cure to anxiety attacks and he didn't even know it!

Holy smokes, I had to try it right away!

I hopped in my Tahoe after meeting with Luke, and I began to try the breathing techniques he taught me.

Take a slow, deep breath (inhale using your nose or mouth) while counting to eight. Concentrate on breathing with your stomach (zero rise of the chest).

Slowly breathe out (exhale) through your mouth on the same eight-second count.

Concentrate on breathing in through your belly and not your chest. When done correctly, you should only see your stomach push out. Your chest should not move at all.

It was working. Just doing this for forty seconds made me feel incredibly calm and collected. I drove off excited to try it out in places where I normally would have panic attacks.

I purposely got in a long line in Publix supermarket just to see how I would do with my breathing strategy. Once an initial bout of panic swept through me, I quietly began my breathing exercises. I watched my stomach go in and out slowly under my t-shirt and felt my body loosen up, my heart rate slow down, and my body temperate slowly drop. All of a sudden, it felt cool in there. My panic was defeated.

Over the next few months, I would put my newfound love of slow stomach breathing to the test in many places. My daughter's school (sandwiched in-between other parents at a play), airport security lines, and a Tampa Bay Lightning game. All of these scenarios that normally would have been incredibly tough for me were now feasible.

Now, does this mean I never experience anxiety or fear? Of course not! Our bodies are wired for fight or flight for a reason. But what I have learned is to avoid panicking. I control my fear, and I OWN my panic attacks so they never bother me again.

I still get a little bit uncomfortable and by no means enjoy being stuck in big crowds where I can't move, but I can do my breathing techniques and never feel the need to flee.

Through all of this, I realized one important piece of the puzzle that MUST go hand in hand with the slow, stomach breathing. **It is simply to believe you can beat it**. If you don't think you can do it, no amount of breathing can save you every time. And that is the cure to defeating any type of fear—not just anxiety attacks. Knowing that you can beat it.

Dan Harris's book, *10% Happier*, further confirmed everything I had learned about breathing. If you don't know the name Dan Harris, you've probably seen him. He has been a well-known anchor and reporter on ABC for many years and was a host on Good Morning America.

Ironically, he first became famous by having a panic attack while on live TV as an anchor and suffered from anxiety and panic attacks as I did for quite some time. On his search for both happiness and a cure for his anxiety, he discovered that controlling his breathing through meditation was the cure. Here is how Dan explained what breathing and meditation did for him:

> *"In moments where I was temporarily able to suspend my monkey mind and simply experience whatever was going on, I got just the smallest taste of the happiness I'd achieved while on retreat."*

Not only did it eliminate panic attacks 100%, but it made him 10% happier as the book title suggests. Strategic breathing, it seems, is a powerful tool for eliminating panic, anxiety, and fear in your life.

BUT, there's something even bigger that you must do.

FACE YOUR FEAR.

The big task comes with facing your biggest fear head on. Facing your biggest fear head on is the toughest part of it all, but once you do, man, you will feel unstoppable! Why? Because facing your fears is where true growth in life happens.

Here is my challenge to you. Face your fear, do your breathing, and promise yourself that you will not flee no matter what. Even if you have a full on panic attack, just sit there and breathe through it knowing that it will pass.

If you can OWN your attack just a couple of times, it won't come back. I still remember the time I first OWNED my panic attack while in a business meeting in Pennsylvania. We were in an old building with a room that was already super hot (which I hate as it brings on sweating, which my mind associates with panic), and I started to feel an attack coming on. Everything in my body was telling me to flee and hit the bathroom, but I was an integral part of the conversation and there was no way I could leave.

So I sat there, breathing slowly through my nose, feeling my body slow down, all while feeling my head get hot, a few sweat beads forming on my forehead. It was like an epic battle between good and evil going on in my body. After no more than thirty seconds, GOOD WON! The attack completely went away, and it was one of the most rewarding things to know I could sit there and OWN it!

IT'S A MINDSET THING

The mind is the most powerful thing God ever created. There is a reason one of the top selling self-help books of all time, *Think and Grow Rich* by Napoleon Hill was 100% about the mind. In that must-read book, he shares story after story of how men became wealthy, miracles happened, and life-changing things were invented all from the mind.

The mind can trick your entire body into believing it is being chased by a lion; it can make a 75-pound anorexic girl believe that she is fat even while she lays in a hospital bed surrounded by doctors telling her she will die if she doesn't eat. The mind can also create the light bulb, it can fool your body into believing it can run a four-minute mile, it can write a book, it can create war, and it can create life. Its possibilities are endless if you program it correctly.

When it comes to conquering fear, you've got to make your brain be on your side. You must **BELIEVE** without a doubt that you can overcome your fears. I unsuccessfully fought panic attacks for so many years because my mind didn't believe I could beat it. In my mind it was just unbeatable, so I became focused on how to tame it when I should have believed I could squash it!

Dr. Nic Lucas was my favorite author from all of the "anxiety books" I read. And he nailed the importance of believing and thinking your way out of it with this quote from his book, *From Anxious To Happy:*

> *"Many people who have anxiety disorder are great thinkers - and they need to learn how to think their way out of anxiety... Sooner or later, you realize that the things you fear in relation to your panic attacks just don't seem to happen. Even though your early warning system is going off, it seems to be a false alarm. Sooner or later, you just have to start questioning your early warning system - and maybe even learn to ignore it."*

One of the greatest masters and programmers of the mind is *Tony Robbins*. I have read most of Tony's books and have listened to his seminars, and they are superb.

In one of his CDs, Tony talks about when tennis player *Andre Agassi* came to him for help. You see, Andre was in the prime of his tennis career, but after numerous grand slam wins, he hit a slump that he couldn't shake.

Tony and Andre started going through some footage of Andre on the court before a game. Tony paused the film as the camera showed both Andre and his opponent looking at each other as they stepped on the court before a final grand slam match.

Tony asked Andre, "What was going through your head right there before the match?"

Andre replied, *"I remember thinking to myself as I looked at the other guy, why did you ever bother to show up? I am going to wipe you all over the court."*

In other words, Andre knew without a doubt that he was going to OWN his opponent!

A couple of hours later, Andre had wiped his opponent all over the court and walked away with a trophy and loads of money.

The next scene that Tony pulled up was a shot of Andre looking at one of his recent opponents right before the match started (it was a match Andre had recently lost). Andre was a much better player than this guy; he outranked him and should have easily been able to win and move on to the next round. But just the opposite happened.

Tony asked Andre, "What was going through your head right there before the match?"

Andre replied, "*I was recalling how bad my backhand was the last time I played him and how many errors I made.*"

Even though Andre was a better player than ever before, was in perfect health, and could beat any tennis player in the world, his mind was holding him back from excellence (and winning Grand Slam tournaments).

Tony worked with Andre to reprogram this mind to get him back to the same level of confidence he had back when he was winning, and it all changed for Andre after that. He went on to win more Grand Slam Tournaments and make more money than ever before. All from a mindset shift.

Another amazing Tony Robbins story came out of one of the books that I listened to multiple times in the car called, **Unleash The Power Within** (a must-buy if you don't already own it). And in that audio book, Tony talks about how rock icon **Bruce Springsteen** gets so nervous before a show that he gets to the point of puking. He goes on to compare how Bruce was dealing with fear versus another celebrity singer he was consulting with.

You see, Tony was working with a well-known female singer who was having a lot of trouble with anxiety and fear in front of her audience. When asked what goes through her mind when she gets anxious, this was her story:

"When I'm about to go on stage, my heart starts racing, my palms start sweating, and I get butterflies in my stomach. I start to get this startling sensation throughout my body, all the way to my fingertips... and that's when I know I'm having a panic attack."

She is completely debilitated and has even canceled shows in the past all due to her panic attacks.

Now compare that with an eerily similar comment that music legend Bruce Springsteen made about what is going on in his head and body right before getting on stage:

"When about to go live, my heart starts racing, my palms start sweating, and I get butterflies in my stomach. I start to get this startling sensation throughout my body, all the way to my fingertips... and that's when I know I'm ready to rock the audience."

You can either let fear control you or you can harness it and ride it to the moon.

I was watching author ***Kamal Ravikant*** speak at the Awesomeness Fest (you can watch it on YouTube—just search Kamal Ravikant Awesomeness Fest), and I loved what he said about conquering his fear of public speaking. Kamal said, *"If something scares me, I know there is magic on the other side when I conquer it. Every single time I have been fearful or scared of something and I had the courage to jump off the cliff and face the fear, magic has happened in my life. Facing your fears is how you sprout new wings."*

Good stuff, and so true.

This chapter promised to help you eliminate anxiety and panic attacks, so here are some of my "pro pointers" on how to defeat it in your own life like I did.

STAY AWAY FROM LOTS OF CAFFEINE!

Caffeine, energy drinks, or anything with tons of sugar will increase your heart rate, which can many times trigger panic if you suffer from this like so many of us. The great news is that it doesn't mean you have to quit drinking coffee. I drink coffee every morning still. But it does mean that you should lay off extreme amounts of caffeine and know that they can trigger panic attacks.

SELF-MEDICATING WITH BOOZE DOESN'T WORK EITHER.

I have found that a single beer or glass of wine can do wonders to taking off a slight edge of anxiety and fear, but you must be able to control your drinking and stop. If you are drinking in the mornings, before work, or before important events, then you have a problem and need to face the reality that you need help.

IT IS CRITICAL THAT YOU GO TO THE PLACE WHERE YOUR PANIC ATTACKS ARE WORST AND OWN IT.

Don't avoid it, walk up to it, laugh at it, and punch it in the face. As psychologist and author M. Scott Peck said in *The Road Less Traveled*, life gets a WHOLE lot better once you face your fears and conquer them. Here is the quote from Scott's awesome book:

> *"Those who have faced their mental illness, accepted total responsibility for it, and made the necessary changes in themselves to overcome it, find themselves not only cured and free from the curses of their childhood*

and ancestry but also find themselves living in a new and different world. What they once perceived as problems they now perceive as opportunities."

TRY YOUR BEST TO AVOID DRUGS TO CURE PANIC ATTACKS OR ANXIETY.

In many cases (but not all), drugs are like putting a Band-Aid on a bullet wound. Always try to alter your mind naturally first, not with drugs. In almost all cases, your mind can be reprogrammed to overcome your fear(s).

BREATHE.

Don't ever forget that it is virtually impossible to have a panic attack when you are 100% relaxed, and your breathing is slow and controlled. Keep breathing through a panic attack, and know that it will pass. A panic attack CANNOT hurt you. A real lion or bear can, however.

Dr. Nic Lucas offered some really helpful words in ***Anxious But Happy***: *"Even if you're concerned about the actual panic attack itself - the simple question is, "what's the worst thing that has ever happened when you've had a panic attack"? They come. They're awful. They go, and you're still there."* I think this is a powerful thing to think about should you find yourself in the midst of an attack.

REALIZE THAT YOU'RE NOT ALONE.

Know that over six million people (just in America) suffer from anxiety attacks every year just like you. You are not weird, and you are not alone. If you feel one coming on and for some reason, the breathing isn't working, tell the people around you that you are having a panic attack. You will be shocked that usually at least one of them has experienced the same thing and will tell you it's ok.

GET THE MOST OUT OF YOUR BREATHING:

- Slowly count to eight (or silently say, "relax") while you breathe in and out. Feel your body slowing down. Feel your heartbeat slow down. Feel your breathing slow down. Concentrate on each breath and watch your stomach go all the way out.
- If you are speaking (like public speaking) and you start to feel a panic attack coming, then slow down your talking, focus on your breath, and don't be afraid to take a couple of deep breaths through your nose while you give the talk.
- Always remember that when your heart rate is slow, and your breathing is controlled, it is virtually impossible to have a panic attack.
- I would also recommend taking one of those weekend freediving courses to learn about your breathing and/or take a meditation class as well. It took me way too long to understand the power and importance of breathing.

Finally, face your fears. Only then can you be truly free. As Kamal says in his first book, **Love Yourself Like Your Life Depends On It**, "*Fighting fear doesn't work. It just drags us in closer. One has to focus on what is real. On the truth. When in darkness, don't fight it. You can't win. Just find the nearest switch, turn on the light.*"

Freedom
Summary/Action Steps

ONE OF THE most important (and overlooked) aspects of control is being in charge of your time. Time is one of the few things that every human on earth gets the same amount of every single day. So, why is it that some people can maximize every waking hour while others seem to get nothing done? It's because most people have little control over their time—and it probably stems from something they've said "yes" to doing.

I love what James Altucher said about the importance of controlling your time in his book, ***The Power Of NO***:

> *"Do you have a tendency to say yes to too many things? If so, try this. You are entitled to three No's for every one Yes in your life… if you don't say yes on your own terms, you are saying it on everyone else's terms, and the results will hurt you."*

Similarly, ***Dan Kennedy*** famously says in his **No B.S.** books, *"If you don't respect and have full control of your own time, don't expect other people to respect it."*

Then there is your emotional life to consider. Another really critical aspect of control is being able to keep anger, hatred, or resentment from taking control of your life. Some books I read such as Kamal Ravikant's,

Live Your Truth, went as far as to say, *"Forgiveness is the key to freedom."* And I have to agree. I mean, have you ever seen a happy person that is constantly holding grudges and angry at the world? Of course not!

Similarly, if you can't control your thoughts, you'll have a tough time being fulfilled in life. That means controlling your emotions, controlling your ability to keep negative thoughts from entering your head, and the ability to keep your mind focused on your mission in life. Almost every book about achieving wealth (from *The Science Of Getting Rich* by Wallace Wattles, to *Think And Grow Rich* by Napoleon Hill, to *The Power Of The Subconscious Mind* by Joseph Murphy) confirms that controlling your thoughts (plus faith) is key to success and long-term happiness.

Finally, you must learn to stand up to your fears and harness that energy into something positive. I love what Stephen Pressfield says about fear is his must-read book, *"The War Of Art."* Here it is:

> *"Are you paralyzed with fear? That's a good sign. Fear is good. Like self-doubt, fear is an indicator. Fear tells us what we have to do. Remember one rule of thumb: the more scared we are of a work or calling, the more sure we can be that we have to do it."*

The biggest lesson you can learn here is to break away from anything that is holding you back or controlling your life! Take risks, learn from your mistakes, and don't let anything control you. Here are just a few things that I have seen control people (including myself), which ultimately take away from your long-term happiness:

- Alcohol
- Anger (or being unable to forgive)
- Drugs
- Money
- A job

- A long commute to a job
- A city
- Food
- Out of control spending
- Cell phone
- Email
- Porn
- Fear
    - Fear of failure
    - Anxiety
- Your boss
- Your house
- Your belongings
- Girlfriend
- Boyfriend
- Spouse
- Parents
- Your thoughts
- Your TIME

It's important that you realize I am not saying you must control every facet of your life. The "control" I am referencing in this chapter is centered on **not letting something control you** more so than you having control over something. Trying to control things out of your control will not do you any good. It's incredibly important that you live life knowing that everything happens for a reason.

Michael Singer really nailed home the power of "going with the flow" and not trying to control every small detail in life with this quote from his top-selling book, *The Surrender Experiment*, in which he writes:

"The universe has been around for 13.8 billion years, and the processes that determine the flow of life around us did not begin when we were

born, nor will they end when we die. What manifests in front of us at any given moment is actually something truly extraordinary - it is the end result of all the forces that have been interacting together for billions of years. We are not responsible for even the tiniest fraction of what is manifesting around us. Nonetheless, we walk around constantly trying to control and determine what will happen in our lives. No wonder there's so much tension, anxiety, and fear. Each of us actually believes that things should be the way we want them, instead of being the natural result of all the forces of creation."

The key is to surrender to the flow of life without giving up control of your life. As Claudia Azula Altucher says in **The Power Of No**, she realized her controlling attitude was sabotaging all of her relationships and, *"The death I needed was to say NO to my relentless obsession to orchestrate every relationship."*

As you can see, control can be a bad thing if you are on the wrong side of the coin.

So how do we strike that balance? Here's a handy formula:

More Control = More Freedom = More Happiness = More Fulfillment

For instance, if you can save 10% of your paycheck (instead of spending 110% of it every month), you have more control of your finances. That choice, in turn, gives you freedom from the stress of living paycheck to paycheck *and* the freedom to use that money toward your goals, which in turn gives you happiness, which in turn leads to fulfillment.

Control also applies to your life, your daily activities, and your schedule. I can recall some of the most stressful (and unhappy) times in my life where I had no control of my schedule. People were bombarding me with emails, texts, and phone calls from eight am to ten pm. I had no life and no control.

But once I finally had the courage to make a rule that I don't answer my phone after six pm, the madness ended. And guess what? I didn't lose any business. I think my customers actually respected me more when I put my foot down and told them I was unreachable after six because of family time.

Scott Adams, the author of **How To Fail At Almost Everything And Still Win Big** (and the creator of **Dilbert**), had this to say about control and happiness: *"A person with a flexible schedule and average resources will be happier than a rich person who has everything except a flexible schedule. Step one in your search for happiness is to continually work toward having control of your schedule."*

Another one I see impacting so many people is the lack of control over your fears and/or anger. When it comes to fear, either you control it, or it controls you. There is no in-between. Same with anger. When you are angry, your brain cannot focus on anything else. You have no control, and you certainly can't be happy and fulfilled when you're mad. Don't let these things control your life.

WHAT ABOUT MEDITATION?

Many of the people that I told about this book before I released it asked about the importance of meditation in the pursuit of happiness. And what I found throughout pretty much every single book I read on happiness was that controlling your breathing, meditation, quiet time, silence, and/or prayer time were all listed at the top in terms of importance.

Tim Ferris interviewed over 200 of the world's most successful people (athletes, authors, billionaires, actors, and icons) in his book, **Tools Of Titans**.

He discovered that *"80% of the world-class performers I've interviewed meditate in the morning in some fashion and the other 20% have meditation-like activities."*

And no, this doesn't mean you have to practice Buddhism, become a monk, or sit in a Zen garden with your legs crossed for hours on end. Meditation can simply be taking the time to shut off your devices, get in a quiet place, and focus on your breathing for 20 minutes. It can mean praying or reflecting for 5-10 minutes in your "Miracle Morning," taking a quiet walk late in the evening or early morning, or just closing your eyes and letting your mind roam free in silence every day.

To be honest, I thought quiet time, breathing techniques, and meditation were some of the hokiest things I had ever heard of until those breathing exercises changed my life by eliminating my panic attacks. And today, my quiet walks outside early in the morning before most of the world is up and trying to distract me are where most of my best ideas and breakthroughs come from.

You still won't see me outside on a yoga mat, cross-legged, with my eyes closed and my hands cupped on my knees in meditation, but I am pleased to admit that I do try to take a 20-minute breathing and clearing of my head break almost every day. My best self seems to come out shortly after my breathing exercises, and I always come out calmer and ready to take on anything. I'd even venture to say that breathing and "silence" in general provides some of the best healing out there.

As you can see, it's the equation at work again.

More Control = More Freedom =
More Happiness = More Fulfillment

Here are some things you can start doing today.

YOUR FREEDOM ACTION STEPS

1. Turn off your cell phone ringer and all potential noises, dings, and beeps TODAY!

   I have had my phone on vibrate for two straight *years* now, and it was a game-changer for my stress and control. And I don't just mean some of the time; I mean 100% of the time. I haven't had a beep, ding, or ringtone come out of my phone in two years except for a morning alarm when I travel. I also recommend deleting your personal email from the phone. Seriously. I did this about a year ago, and my stress levels have never been so low. And guess what? I haven't missed a single emergency or anything important yet! I check my personal email once per day (in the evening), and it was one of my best decisions ever.

   And if you think that sounds too hard, wait until you hear what Bert and John Jacobs, the founders of *Life is Good* revealed in their book by the same name. They completely deleted their email accounts. As in gone forever. No way to email them! And they said it was one of the most liberating things they ever did. If you aren't familiar with the Life Is Good brand, it is a $100 million company that started from a "Life Is Good" t-shirt. So if the founder and CEO of a $100 million company can delete his entire email account and still get by, then I am certain you can at least take your personal email account off of your phone.

2. Go through each of the following controlling factors below and pick the one that has the most control over you or the one that is eating up too much of your resources. If there is one not listed that you think is controlling you and keeping you from long-term happiness, then pick that one instead.

- Fear
- Anger
- Job
- Spouse or loved one
- Health
- Eating
- Spending
- House, cars, toys, or other payments/debt that control you
- Alcohol, drugs, etc.

After you have picked the one that is negatively affecting you the most, start writing down a 30-day, 60-day, 90-day, and one-year goal for this controlling issue. Write out exactly how much your life will improve when you control this issue. Envision how good it will feel when you start controlling it. Include the steps on how you plan on eliminating and controlling it instead of it controlling you. Then, take action!

Repeat one at a time with any other significant issues on the list.

3. Face your BIGGEST FEAR today!
4. Remember that everything you have in life is RENTED. Make the best use of it.
5. Live within your means. Only buy stuff you can afford to pay cash for (minus your home)
6. Give 10% (or more) of your income away every month
7. BREATHE!

Cornerstone #3

Love

Love

Overview

Houston, we have a problem.

My wife and I were living in a beautiful townhome in downtown Houston. I was making more money than ever before, she was finishing up her residency to become a full-fledged eye surgeon, and we had a beautiful, healthy baby girl that we adored. From the outside looking in, life was glorious.

But in reality, we were quite the opposite of glorious. We were borderline miserable.

Loren was working crazy hours, I was traveling quite a bit, and all of our "spare time" was spent catching up with each other and taking walks with the baby. We didn't have time for friends anymore, we didn't have time for church, and we didn't have time for our kickball team. I'm almost embarrassed to say that we pretty much had zero connections within our community—unless you count waving to your neighbors as community-centric.

We found time for ourselves and nothing else, and we were miserable because of it.

What went wrong?

Before I reveal the big problem, let's go back in time a handful of years to when I was facing a different, but similar issue.

I woke up one morning with a pounding headache, wondering, "Where the heck am I?"

As I looked around through bloodshot eyes, I recognized that I was in my brand new monstrous master bedroom.

When I slowly stumbled downstairs, I saw people strewn all over the place. My friends were passed out on the couch, in my guest room, in my kitchen, and all over the basement. One guy slept in my walk-in pantry, and a co-worker of mine was zonked out in my laundry room on top of the washer and dryer! I took a look out the window and saw more carnage. There were people still sleeping outside in their cars, and I watched as one of my neighbors gently poked at my friend who was snoring on the pavement right behind a parked car.

"Now that's how you throw a party!" I laughed, feeling pretty proud of myself.

Do you remember the big house in Bridgemill I told you about earlier? Well, this was the "breaking in the new home" party. I had friends galore show up! Work friends, friends from college, and even many of my close fraternity brothers came up for the bash. Most of the neighbors came by to meet me as well, and all counted there were well over two hundred people that made their way into my home that night. I was the hit of the community for sure! It was such a rush to show off my new house to so many friends, and I was so high on life that I didn't even care about the new hole in my wall from the late-night festivities.

It felt amazing to share my new home with so many people. Life was good.

But my excitement dwindled as one by one my friends picked themselves up and left. Now that it was empty, my house felt huge, cavernous and, most of all, quiet. That is how it would feel most nights since there was just one person living in it. ME.

Before buying this home, I had recently come out of a very serious relationship with a girl whom I thought I was going to marry. I guess I thought the answer to getting over the tough breakup was to buy a huge house and try to hook up with as many girls as I could. But it turns out that both decisions left me feeling pretty empty and lonely.

Can you guess what this scenario has in common with the unhappiness I was feeling in Houston?

It was a lack of *love* in my life.

And I'm not just talking about romance. As we discuss love in the next few chapters, it's important that you don't confuse "love" with romance, as the two don't always go hand in hand. I am talking about a slightly different definition of love. We'll be looking at the three kinds of love that are critical to your happiness in life.

Over the course of my reading and research, I found that the most fulfilled people in the world had a healthy balance of three different types of love in their life:

- Love within a family (spouse/kids/significant other/immediate family)
- Love within a community (friendships, relationships, a common tribe)
- Loving yourself

Jason Fischer sums up all three forms of love in one paragraph of his book, ***The Two Truths About Love***:

> *"Everything boils down to relationships. Relationships are at the very heart of human experience. We are all constantly relating: with partners or lovers, family members, pets, strangers, and friends; at work or school; with every aspect of our environment – the weather, traffic, current events, our finances, and so on; and with ourselves, our regrets or resentments about the past, our hopes or dreams for the future, and our dissatisfactions, both small and large, about our current situation, who we are or are not, and what we don't have. From this complex matrix of interwoven relationships, the entirety of our suffering and joy arises."*

Let's discuss each form of love in it's own chapter.

10

Love Within A Family

I GREW UP in a small town, smack dab in the middle of Florida called Winter Haven. If you took a thumbtack to a map and tried to pin it on "the middle of Florida," your tack would certainly land on or near Winter Haven (or perhaps Haines City if you are really accurate). Although today Winter Haven now boasts one of the only two LEGOLANDs in America, when I was growing up there were more orange trees than people. (That's probably still true today, too.)

Some people love the small town feel, the lack of traffic, being able to walk into a shop or restaurant where everyone knows each other (and each other's business), or going to the town's only movie theatre on the weekend and running into everyone you know. But not me. I had the itch to get out of Winter Haven as fast as I could. I prided myself on being "independent, " and I dreamed of living in a big city with tons of things to do, along with unlimited possibilities.

My family had no idea why I would ever want such a thing. Given that almost every single one of our relatives lived in Winter Haven, the thought of moving away had never occurred to them. Both sets of my grandparents were within a handful of miles from us, most of my aunts, uncles, and cousins lived nearby, and even both sets of my great-grandparents lived in Winter Haven before they passed away.

I guess you could say I was the black sheep because the thought of being so close to my family bugged me. I found it odd that none of them dreamed of conquering the world like I did—they weren't even that interested in seeing much of it. I found it disappointing that none of them had the adventuresome spirit that I had to travel and to live in a new city. Quite honestly, I found myself wondering what kind of redneck family I had been born into that always wants to stop over and share stories and hang out.

And then I spent my first Thanksgiving alone in my big ol' house on the golf course.

I may have been patting myself on my back for my tough-as-nails work ethic and independence as I proudly told my parents that I was too busy to make it home for Thanksgiving that year. But it didn't take long for me to realize how lonely I was without my family.

I was surprised, to be honest. I had been going at a hundred miles per hour with my job, and that made it easy to forget about how much I love surrounding myself with people I care about. I completely forgot how *good* it feels. Now that I had finally taken a break and slowed down, I realized how empty my life was without family and loved ones around.

I finally understood why our family stuck together. I had proudly told friends and colleagues that no one in our immediate or extended family had ever gone through a divorce (which is still true to this day as far as I know), but I never put two and two together to figure out why our family was such an anomaly these days.

From that day forward, I started to appreciate my tight-knit clan more and more. I'd get excited about coming home for holidays. Not only that, I looked at my family and relatives through a different lens. It finally made sense why none of them ever got divorced. Family = Support = Love = Staying Power.

You might be thinking, "Sure. Great, Joe, but I don't need to you tell me that family is important. That's a given." That's what I thought too. But trust me, there is *plenty* to learn here. Let's break it down into the most important parts of the books I have read. To begin, let's talk about marriage and how it interacts with happiness.

HAPPY MARRIAGE, HAPPY LIFE

Book after book, and study after study proved that in general, married people are more content and happy in life than non-married or divorced people. Now, although I certainly know married people that are miserable, even celibate monks like the Dalai Lama had quotes like this about marriage from *The Art Of Happiness*:

> *"There have been literally thousands of studies and surveys that prove Americans and Europeans who are married are happier and more satisfied with life than single or widowed people – or especially compared to divorced or separated people. One survey found that six in ten Americans who rate their marriage as "very happy" also rate their life as a whole as "very happy."*

Does that mean you can't be happy or fulfilled if you aren't married? Of course not! And it certainly doesn't mean that just because you get married you will be happier either. I've seen a lot of people marry the wrong guy or gal and the relationship made both of them miserable (until they got a divorce).

But the Dalai Lama's words—and the pile of studies backing them up—do reveal just how much of an impact an intimate relationship can have on your happiness. The reason married people (in general) are happier is that the most intimate relationship you can have is a partner that you share a home with, confide in, and with whom you build a life every day.

Tal Ben-Shahar has this to say about happiness and relationships in his book, **Happier**: *"While relationships in general are important for the ultimate currency, romantic relationships reign supreme. Summarizing the research on well being, David Myers acknowledges that "there are few stronger predictions of happiness than a close, nurturing, intimate, lifelong companionship with one's best friend."*

In fact, the importance of intimate relationships goes all the way back to the story of Adam and Eve, and it can be seen throughout history when you look at happy and fulfilled people. One thing they all have in common is intimate and special relationships in their life. And when you combine the close relationship with mutual goals and desires in life, it is powerful stuff.

But if that is true then why do so many "romantic and passionate relationships" end up in divorce or separation?

Social psychologist, **Ellen Berscheid** from the University of Minnesota, concluded that it was *"the failure to appreciate the half-life of passionate love that dooms a relationship."* In other words, relationships built solely on passion (aka sex and passionate love) rarely last long and keep couples fulfilled. Ironically, we all know this to be true, yet countless people keep making bad marriage decisions thinking "this one is different" and that they will find a way to work things out. Wrong! Don't get into a serious relationship with someone that is based solely on sex. It never works out.

Likewise, the **Dalai Lama** said this regarding the endless pursuit of romantic love that so many of us are fooled into by watching movies and reading fictional love stories: *"It's something (never-ending romantic love) that is based on fantasy, unattainable, and therefore may be a source of frustration. So, on that basis it cannot be seen as a positive thing. I think that if one is seeking to build a truly satisfying relationship, the best way of bringing this about is to get to* *know the deeper nature of the person and relate to her or him on that level, instead of merely on the basis of superficial characteristics."*

In other words, don't believe everything you see in the movies and read in the tabloid magazines about beautiful and famous people. *My wise mom* told me growing up, *"Before you marry someone, ask yourself if you would still be madly in love with them if they got in a bad accident tomorrow and ended up in a wheelchair for life. If the answer isn't a 100% confident 'Yes,' then move on."*

Tal Ben-Sharar had this to say about the movie myth in **Happier**: *"The problem is that movies end where love begins. It's the living happily ever after that poses the greatest challenge; it's after the sun sets that difficulties often arise."*

So what is the key to a happy romantic relationship? Tal Ben-Sharar nails it with this quote, *"Unconditional love is the foundation of a happy relationship."* Ironically, unconditional love is exactly what we all swear to do (and even sign our names to on our marriage license) when we get married, yet half of us throw the promises out the window when things get tough.

It's also critical to point out that a relationship with a spouse will not solve all of your problems. As we will discuss shortly, you must love yourself before a soul mate can have much of a long-term impact. Eckhart Tolle had this to say about love in his book, **The Power Of Now**:

"Never before have relationships been as problematic and conflict ridden as they are now. As you may have noticed, they are not here to make you happy or fulfilled. If you continue to pursue the goal of salvation through a relationship, you will be disillusioned time and time again. But if you accept that the relationship is here to make you conscious instead of happy, then the relationship will offer you salvation, and you will be aligning yourself with the higher consciousness that wants to be born into this world."

Scott Peck spells this out even further with this powerful quote from **The Road Less Traveled**: *"When you require another individual for your survival, you are a parasite on that individual. There is no choice, no freedom involved in your relationship. It is a matter of necessity rather than love. Love is the free exercise of choice. Two people love each other only when they are quite capable of living without each other but choose to live with each other."*

Spot on.

Another key to a happy and long-lasting marriage is listening. Listening is giving someone your full attention. And giving someone your full attention is love. Thus listening is love. Here is what Scott Peck says about it: *"Since true listening is love in action, nowhere is it more appropriate than in marriage. Yet most couples never truly listen to each other."*

I know I've been guilty of looking at my phone while my wife talks to me. How about you?

THE POWER OF PRAYER

The third and final tip to a long-lasting and happy marriage is prayer. The power of prayer (both with couples and individuals) showed up in numerous books including, **The Power Of Positive Thinking** by Norman Vincent Peale, **Think And Grow Rich** by Napoleon Hill, **The Purpose Driven Life** by Rick Warren, and the obvious, **Couples Who Pray: The Most Intimate Act Between A Man And A Woman** by Squire Rushnell and Louise DuArt.

A few quotes from **The Power Of Positive Thinking** reveal just a few of the benefits of prayer in a relationship:

"Every problem can be solved and solved right if you pray. Prayer is the greatest power available to the individual in solving his personal problems... prayer is the manifestation of energy... prayer driven deeply

into your subconscious mind can remake you. It releases and keeps power flowing freely. It is important to realize that you are dealing with the most tremendous power in the world when you pray... where God and love are, there is happiness."

Likewise, the **Bible** makes it abundantly clear that believing and trusting in God leads to love as stated in 1 John 4:16, *"God is love. Whoever lives in love lives in God, and God in them."*

Regardless of whether you pray silently, out loud, in church, at home, at work, or through meditation, prayer is proven to work wonders. Period.

Let's move on to kids.

DO KIDS MAKE YOU HAPPIER?

If you have children, then you know that kids can be incredibly rewarding, yet brutally tough at the same time. Your life changes when you have kids. Your priorities change. The way you look at the world changes (among other things like your waistline, hairline, your patience, and your sleep patterns).

Throughout all of the books I read, there was nothing that specifically said kids equal happiness and fulfillment, but it was clear that leaving a legacy on your deathbed does. So for some of us, our legacy is our children and grandchildren. For others, it is something else. Think about people like Jesus, Mother Teresa, or the Dalai Lama. It could easily be said that their driving purpose in life was bigger than anything having offspring could have done. Certainly, no one would argue that they left behind a powerful and long-lasting legacy.

Your legacy is 100% self-determined. It is whatever you choose to make it. Perhaps you want to pass on your wealth to an amazing cause or start your own foundation that will continue to live and impact people for years after your death. Or perhaps part of your mission is teaching kids music, sports, religion, art, or how to read.

At the same time, don't fool yourself into letting money or some other driving factor prevent you from having kids. Later in this book you will hear the top five things that people regret on their deathbed. Guess what? Not a single one of them ever said they wished they didn't have children or said, "I wish my family were smaller." Children might drive you crazy and make you forfeit some (if not all) freedom for a couple of years, but it pays big dividends down the road. And that is the best way to look at having children. A long-term investment in your legacy.

Finally, don't ever be the man or woman that sacrifices starting a family for your job. Jobs come and go. Jobs mean nothing when you die. Your family, your legacy, and your life's mission are all that matter during your final days on this earth.

KIDS, HAPPINESS, AND MENTAL DISORDERS

While reading M. Scott Peck's **The Road Less Traveled**, I came across a quote about the powerful legacy of love with kids, and couldn't get it out of my head. Here's what he said: *"For the most part, mental illness is caused by an absence of or defect in the love that a particular child required from its particular parents for a successful maturation and spiritual growth."*

Meaning, as a parent, you are creating a living legacy every single day with your kids. The way you interact with them, care for them, and what you model for them can create lasting impact in their lives for better or worse.

Similarly, Norman Vincent Peale had this to say in **The Power Of Positive Thinking**:

"I was interested to read a statement by a psychologist that infants can "catch" fear and hatred from people around them more quickly than they can catch measles or other infection diseases. The virus of fear may burrow deeply into their subconsciousness and remain there for a lifetime. But, adds the psychologist, fortunately infants can also catch love and goodness and faith and so grow up to be normal, healthy children and adults."

Norman goes on to add, *"Dr. Franklin Ebaugh of the University of Colorado Medical School maintains that one third of all cases of illness in general hospitals are clearly organic in nature and onset, one third are a combination of emotional and organic, and one third are clearly emotional."* In other words, large portions of people sitting in hospitals are suffering from a lack of love and a lack of positive thinking.

Love. Pretty powerful stuff.

I'll leave you with three final tips from a highly shared blog post regarding making the most of your time on Earth. The blog post is by Tim Urban, and it's titled, ***"The Tail End"*** (just Google "Tim Urban Wait But Why The Tail End").

In his post, Tim laid out how much time we have left with our loved ones using some really hard-hitting infographics. After factoring in the actual time that he currently spends with his own parents, here is what Tim realized after plotting out future "in-person together time" with his parents assuming everyone lives to age 90 (note that Tim is only in his 30s).

"It turns out that when I graduated from high school, I had already used up 93% of my in-person parent time. I'm now enjoying the last 5% of that time. We're in the tail end."

Guess what? He's not alone. Have you ever thought about how many encounters and how much real time you have left with the people you love? If your family members or loved ones live in a different city, state, or country than you, it is shocking how little in-person time you really have left with them. This blog post was a real eye-opener for me personally. Really makes you appreciate being around the people you love. Here are Tim's three main takeaways from his research:

Setting aside my secret hope that technological advances will let me live to 700, I see three takeaways here:

*1) **Living in the same place as the people you love matters.** I probably have 10X the time left with the people who live in my city as I do with the people who live somewhere else.*

*2) **Priorities matter.** Your remaining face time with any person depends largely on where that person falls on your list of life priorities. Make sure this list is set by you—not by unconscious inertia.*

*3) **Quality time matters.** If you're in your last 10% of time with someone you love, keep that fact in the front of your mind when you're with them and treat that time as what it actually is: precious.*

11

Love Within A Community

THINK BACK TO the late 90s for a second…

Do you recall what was happening in the "pop music" world?

I sure do. It ended up costing me a lot of money, BUT at the same time, it opened my eyes to something I never really understood. Let me explain in this funny (and true) story.

My best friend Doug and I set our alarms to wake us up at seven am the next morning. We were giddy about heading over to the Georgia Tech campus the next morning to buy Backstreet Boys concert tickets.

No lie.

You see, Georgia Tech had recently installed one of the fastest Ethernet lines in the entire country, and if you wanted to get front row seats to Britney Spears, the Backstreet Boys, or the up and coming group 'N Sync, you had to have the fastest Internet out there. At Georgia Tech, we did. Plus we were competing against moms and teenagers with dial-up modems. They didn't stand a chance.

The next morning, we jolted awake at the sound of our alarms, threw clothes on, and made it to a line of computers inside one of Tech's computer labs. We logged into www.Ticketmaster.com, and waited anxiously for 8:00 am to arrive.

As soon as the clock hit 7:59, we both started refreshing the screen over and over again waiting for it to show that the Backstreet Boys tickets were available. Being on one of the fastest Internet connections in the nation, we both got in right at 8:00, and we secured four front row seats to their upcoming concert in Orlando. Doug and I started licking our chops and high-fiving. "We are about to make so much money!"

You see, we had no intention of actually going to the show. In fact, I wouldn't be caught dead at a Backstreet Boys concert. Quite honestly, I didn't understand why people liked concerts at all. I was content listening to music at home with no crowds, no long lines for the bathroom, and "unlimited" beer. Forget about a stadium of screaming teenagers. But I did know one thing: these crazy fans would pay big money for our tickets.

Our plan was simple. Use Georgia Tech's super-fast Ethernet system to buy seats up front (preferably front row) for popular concerts (like Britney Spears and the boy bands), list the tickets on *eBay* for four to six times what we paid for them, and watch our bank accounts grow. For the first couple of times, it worked brilliantly. Doug and I made some sweet cash from "the crazy people" willing to pay hundreds per seat to see five guys dance around in goofy outfits.

But then a different type of crazy entered our life. Some lady was furious that we were making so much money selling these concert tickets, and she wanted to teach us a lesson. So she started bidding upwards of $15,000 per ticket (that she never intended on paying). At first, we were blown away when we saw the offer in our *eBay* auction, but we quickly realized this lady was trying to kill our auction. We kept booting her off the auction, but she kept rebidding. She did this numerous times as we watched the clock tick down in our auction.

The auction ended. She beat us at our own "fast Internet" game by getting her bid in at the last second. We just sold four Backstreet Boys tickets for $60,000 total to a person that had no intention of paying for them. Here was the kicker. Back then, **eBay** charged the seller 2.5% for anything they sold—IMMEDIATELY! They charged my credit card for the full amount, even though we never got paid).

So as things stood, my credit card was now maxed out with $1,500 that I didn't have, and to make matters worse, we were still stuck with four Backstreet Boys tickets. Long story short, they had to investigate the whole deal. We eventually got our money back (and a slap on the wrist for scalping tickets), and we ended up selling those seats just slightly above face value. Just like that, our brilliant business plan was done. We never scalped concert tickets again. We were out of that business. As 'N Sync would say, *"Baby, Bye, Bye, Bye, Bye, Bye."*

Now, you might be wondering, what does all of this have to do with love within a community?

TRIBES

Ever wonder why there are millions of associations, clubs, and other affinity groups in America? Have you ever wondered why tens of thousands of people will pack in an outdoor stadium in the middle of Wisconsin during sub-zero temps to cheer on a football team (or pay crazy amounts of money to see the Backstreet Boys)? And have you ever wondered why millions will take off work every year and drive hundreds of miles to attend biker rallies?

It's because we all crave a sense of belonging to something. We crave strong communities. We crave Tribes.

As Seth Godin explains in his book, ***Tribes***, *"Tribes give us something to believe in. Tribes are about faith – about belief in an idea and in a community.*

And they are grounded in respect and admiration for the leader of the tribe and for the other members as well."

Seth goes on to reveal later in the book that, *"Caring is the key emotion at the center of the tribe. Tribe members care what happens, to their goals and to one another."* Tribes are a community. Tribes are a different form of love.

To bring all this back in full circle, recall that I still didn't understand why people enjoyed concerts so much. The main reason was I had only been to one concert in my life, and that was to see *Alabama* at the Strawberry Festival when I was really young. Yet, within that same twelve-month period of the Backstreet Boys saga, I attended my very first concert as a young adult and learned about this "unseen power of a community/tribe" firsthand. The concert was *Jimmy Buffett*, and I got indoctrinated into what it means to be a "Parrothead."

If you've been to a Jimmy Buffet concert, then you know what I'm talking about. Everyone is happy, everyone is friendly and smiles at each other, and magic starts to happen when tens of thousands of people all gather together for a common love—in this case, singing "Cheeseburger in Paradise." Regardless of whether we're talking about Jimmy Buffett, The Grateful Dead, the opening night of the latest Star Wars movie, or Sunday service, when a community of people comes together for a shared reason it's a powerful thing.

Seth Godin nails it again with this quote about the power of a tribe as he talks about what *The Grateful Dead* did to the music industry:

"They didn't succeed by selling records – they only had one Top 40 album. Instead, they succeeded by attracting and leading a tribe.

"Human beings can't help it: we need to belong. One of the most powerful of our survival mechanisms is to be part of a tribe, to contribute to (and

take from) a group of like-minded people. We are drawn to leaders and to their ideas, and we can't resist the rush of belonging and the thrill of new."

So after my first (of many) Jimmy Buffett concerts, I finally understood the power of love within a community. Why? Because that is exactly what happens when you get a group of people together for a common cause: magic and love.

And concerts are just the tip of the iceberg when it comes to the power of communities. I am sure we can all agree that most of us tend to hang around with people that share similar goals, desires, beliefs, and loves as we do. Whether it is a concert, an association, a club, a church, or a synagogue, we have a burning desire to be around people that share our same beliefs, values, and even fears. Why?

"Humans are social animals. There are probably dozens of ways we absorb energy, inspiration, skills, and character traits from those around us," says Dilbert founder Scott Adams in his top-selling book, **How To Fail At Almost Everything And Still Win Big**. Scott continues with this awesome quote:

"Given our human impulse to pick up the habits and energy of others, you can use that knowledge to literally program your brain the way you want. Simply find the people who most represent what you would like to become and spend as much time with them as you can without trespassing, kidnapping, or stalking. Their good habits and good energy will rub off on you."

On the same subject, New York Times bestselling author Daniel Gilbert wrote this in his book, **Stumbling on Happiness**: *"If I wanted to predict your happiness and I could only know one thing about you, I wouldn't want to know your gender, religion, health, or income. I'd want to know about the strength of your relationships with your friends and family."*

Similarly, numerous books and leaders discuss the idea (first heard by motivational speaker *Jim Rohn*) that you become the average of your five closest friends. In most cases, this becomes true regarding wealth, looks, the size of your house, the amount of kids you have, your age, etc. Give it a shot and analyze yourself compared to your five closest friends. Are you in the middle when you compare yourself to them?

Likewise, in **Happier,** Tal Ben-Shahar reveals a study done by *"Ed Diener and Martin Seligman, two of the leading positive psychologists, who studied "very happy people" and compared them to those who were less happy."* Can you guess the one big difference between them? *"The only external factor that distinguished the two groups was the presence of "rich and satisfying social relationships."*

Community is an essential part of happiness. And it makes sense. We thrive on the energy and love from other people around us. Loneliness and being separated from those we care about, on the other hand, can be terrifying.

Psychoanalyst and social philosopher **Erich Fromm** was known for preaching that a human's most basic fear in life is the threat of being separated from other humans. He proposed that being separated from loved ones (starting in infancy when a baby first shows signs of separation anxiety) is the main source of all anxiety in human life.

Howard Cutler (author of **The Art Of Happiness** with the Dalai Lama) discussed a study that was done at Duke University Medical Center where they found that heart disease patients who weren't married or didn't have a close confidant were three times more likely to die within five years of the diagnosis compared to patients with the exact same diagnosis who were married or had a best friend.

A similar study that went on for nine years proved that people with more social support and close relationships had lower death rates and lower rates of cancer compared to people with few relationships (aka loners).

Pretty powerful stuff! Don't ever forget that social connections and relationships are one of the most important drivers of your happiness.

Even Rich Koch's business book, ***The 80/20 Principle*** (where Rich proves everything in business and personal life follows the 80/20 rule - for instance, 20% of your friends most likely receive 80% of your time and love while 80% of your friends get the remaining 20% of your time and love), had this to say about the power of relationships:

"Without relationships we are either dead to the world or dead. Although banal, this is true: our friendships are at the heart of our lives."

Finally, don't dismiss the power of listening when it comes to love within a family, group, community, or while one-on-one with someone. Just like listening to a spouse or child is one of the best ways to show your love, the same goes for your community or tribe.

Famous psychiatrist M. Scott Peck, MD had this to say about the importance of listening in ***The Road Less Traveled***: *"The principal form that the work of love takes is attention. When we love another we give him or her our attention; we attend to that person's growth. And by far the most common and important way in which we can exercise our attention is by listening."*

Can you guess what all of the best psychiatrists (aka "love doctors") do during their sessions with unhappy and unbalanced clients? They listen. They ask questions and get their patient talking. They show that they care by giving their full attention to the other person (which is the ultimate form of love). Scott goes on to say, *"It is the patient's sense that he or she is being listened to, often for the first time in years, and perhaps the first time ever."*

Being the recipient of someone's full attention is a rare thing, especially in the age of the smartphone, and that makes it highly valuable.

COMPASSION AND GIVING BACK

Have you ever met someone who came back from helping build a home with Habitat for Humanity, volunteering at an orphanage, or serving food in a soup kitchen and said, "Man, what a waste of time that was!" Of course not! There is something magical that occurs in our mind and body when we give back, when we give to the less fortunate, and when we share our time, money, and energy with other people.

Deepak Chopra dedicates an entire chapter called the "Law of Giving" in his book, *The Seven Spiritual Laws Of Success*. Here is what Deepak has to say in the book:

> *"The best way to put the Law of Giving into operation – to start the whole process of circulation – is to make a decision that any time you come into contact with anyone, you will give them something. It doesn't have to be in the form of material things; it could be a flower, a compliment, or a prayer. In fact, the most powerful forms of giving are non-material. The gifts of caring, attention, affection, appreciation, and love are some of the most precious gifts you can give, and they don't cost you anything."*

Research has proven that compassionate and giving people tend to be happier, healthier, more popular, and are more successful in life. One study even showed how everyone from the elderly, to alcoholics, to people living with AIDS, showed significant improvement in health if they did volunteer work while getting treatment. Pretty wild, huh?

And do you want to know the one thing that every single super successful person I read about such as Walt Disney, Steve Jobs, or John

Rockefeller had in common? It was that they all consistently gave away money. Loads of money in fact. It has been expressed by countless people that every time they give away money with nothing expected in return, it mysteriously came back to them tenfold down the road. Sometimes it came back to them instantaneously in the form of money, and sometimes it came back years later in some other positive form. But it always seemed to be a cycle of good things coming back to those who share.

Here's what Rich Devos (founder of Amway) had to say about giving in *Simply Rich*:

> *"Looking back at eighty-eight years of life, I believe one principle rises above the others. People who achieve the highest levels of success—whether in business or in raising families or simply in discovering fulfillment and satisfaction and purpose in life—are those who place their focus on other people rather than themselves. I have succeeded only by helping others succeed."*

I was recently in Bok Tower Gardens with my dad, brother, and two daughters, and I came across this amazing quote by *Edward Bok*, considered one of the best philanthropists to ever live in central Florida. Bok said, *"Give to the world the best you have and the best will come back to you."* Powerful stuff.

One of the best "happiness exercises" I've ever tried was something I started testing out after I read *Tools Of Titans*, by Tim Ferriss. The particular happiness exercise was introduced to Tim from his podcast guest, Chade-Meng Tan, a best-selling author and one Google's first employees.

Here's the exercise: *"Identify two human beings and think to yourself, "I wish for this person to be happy." This is the joy of loving-kindness,"* says Chade-Meng. *"It turns out that being on the giving end of a kind thought is rewarding in and of itself... All other things being equal, to increase your happiness, all you have to do is randomly wish for someone else to be happy. That is all. It basically takes no time and no effort."*

During a speaking engagement Chade-Meng challenged his audience to take it one step further by doing the following once they went back to work the next day: *"Once an hour, every hour, randomly identify two people walking past your office and secretly wish for each one of them to be happy."* One of the people in that audience sent Chade-Meng an email the week after his speech that read, *"I hate my job. I hate coming to work every single day. But I attended your talk on Monday, did the homework on Tuesday, and Tuesday was my happiest day in 7 years."*

Dan Kennedy's books had a really big impact on my business (and personal) life. In one of his books, **The No B.S. Guide To Wealth Attraction**, he shared a tip that he claimed changed his life, changed the lives of many others, and gave him much fulfillment. It changed my life as well. Want to know what it was?

Here is what Dan encourages every single one of his clients to do: open up a brand new saving or checking account, and anytime you get a paycheck or make any money, put 10% of your take-home income into that savings account. NO MATTER WHAT.

Note that this 10% is after any 401(k) contributions, deductions, and taxes. The only rule for this account is that you can't spend it on yourself. You must find ways to give 100% of the money away. It could be to your church, to someone in need, to a charity, or anyone or anything that you could impact positively with those funds.

I'll be honest, it was really easy for me to go to my bank and open the new account. It was even easy for me to put the minimum $250 into the account to get it opened. But it was **incredibly hard and painful** to part ways with 10% of my income. Heck, most people are trying to save 10% of their paycheck, and here Dan Kennedy is telling me to take an extra 10% and give it away with nothing in return.

Well, I finally started doing it, and at first I just watched the account slowly grow. To be honest, in the back of my head I was telling myself that I could use it for an emergency or something. I did not want to give this money away! But I stayed true to the cause. Before you know it, this new account had a few thousand bucks in it! I still didn't know who (or what) I was going to give this money to, so I just waited until the right moment.

That same week I was catching up with my parents, and they mentioned that their church was getting a bit low on funds. My dad said they could really use a couple thousand dollars this month to pay some bills. This was the same church I had attended all through junior high and high school, and although I hadn't been in many years (minus a couple of Christmas services), I felt like this was my chance to make an impact. You see, their church is a small, tight-knit community with many elderly people, and I can only assume that many members of the church probably don't tithe $2,000 for the entire year. And here I was, ready to cut a check for $2,000 to a church I hadn't been to in years.

I slept on it one more night to make sure no other opportunities came up (or perhaps it was my last ditch effort to hold on to the money for one more day). But the following day I wrote out a check for $2,000 and threw it in the mail to surprise my parent's church. You know, it was the weirdest thing when I did it. It felt amazing to cut that check and mail it off. I remember smiling ear to ear as I put it in our mailbox while envisioning their pastor opening up the mail and seeing a $2,000 surprise check from someone he hadn't seen or talked to in years. I don't think at any time in my life I had received so much satisfaction from giving away money.

And then the wildest thing happened just a short time later. I received an email from a guy's assistant that I had done a joint webinar with over forty days earlier. He had promised me that he would give me a referral fee for any of my customers that signed up with him, but we had nothing in writing, and quite honestly, I didn't expect much. I liked the guy doing the webinar, and I knew that he would add value to my customers from all of the fantastic tips he gives away in his webinars.

But here is what the surprise email read: *"It has been 30 days since we processed credit cards from the joint webinar we did (thus the "free look period" was up), and you have a check coming for $11,600 for the referrals that came from the webinar. Please let us know the best address to send it to and who to make the check out to."*

Holy smokes!!!

Over $11,000 just walked into my life just like that. And I have numerous other stories just like this every time I give money away. Now I don't tell you this so you start giving away your money in hopes that you will get surprise checks, because that isn't always the case. But what is always the case is how fulfilled you will feel when you contribute your money or time to people or groups in need. As **Zig Ziglar** said, *"You will get all you want in life if you help enough other people get what they want."*

You can even do a bunch of small things like surprising people in the military by paying for their meal when you see them eating in the airport, giving a surprise big tip to a waiter that shared his or her big dreams with you, or creating an unforgettable Christmas for a family that can't afford to buy presents for their kids.

And remember that it doesn't have to be money. Love currency can be time, attention, a smile, and even prayer. The best news is that it's free to smile at people, free to strike up a conversation with a new person, and free to give an old friend a hug.

Find your tribe. Love your community. Care about others. Give back.

12

Love Yourself

Girls.

There must be something seriously wrong with them.

How do I know?

Well, it certainly couldn't be my fault that I couldn't hold onto a serious girlfriend while in my twenties.

I was a solid catch, after all! I was in the best shape of my life, I had a good job, I knew how to make people laugh, and I was a pretty popular guy (despite my ongoing battle with anxiety). What was wrong with these girls I was dating?

Wrong question, right? What I should have been asking was what was wrong with me?

Unfortunately, I didn't see my serious flaw until it was too late. But then again, everything happens for a reason.

Want to know happened? Let me tell you my quick story.

After countless dates, flings, and short-term relationships, I finally found an amazing girl that I believed could be "the one." Her name was Katie, and like many new relationships, we spent the first six months or so of our relationship in pure bliss. No real fights, no drama, all good times.

And then *"it"* happened. I began to get jealous of other guys looking at and talking to Katie. I began to get jealous if she wanted to have a girl's night out. I became argumentative about anything and everything that came in-between Katie and I. Before I knew it, my urge to control my girlfriend was getting out of control, and you can only imagine what happened next.

The *"it"* I described above was my feeling the need to have control, but if you dig a couple of layers deeper, it came down to me not loving myself. I didn't understand this until many years later when I met my soon-to-be wife. I knew I wanted to marry this girl named Loren that I was dating, and I was dead set on not making the same mistakes I made with Katie.

After evaluating my past relationships, two things became incredibly evident in all of my failed attempts at love. One, my controlling and jealous attitude, and two, the fact that I didn't like what I had become inside. And every single time, those two things manifested themselves in my need for control.

It was like a drug. I truly hated how it made me feel and what it was doing to my relationships, but at the same time I couldn't free myself of it. I was a control addict. And the problem stemmed from me not truly loving myself. And it sure didn't help that I kept making the false assumption that being loved by someone else would make it all better. Boy, was I wrong.

When I read **The Road Less Traveled**, by M. Scott Peck, it became abundantly clear how dependent I was on others to try and make me happy.

No wonder I couldn't keep a girlfriend. Here is what Scott says about it in the book:

> "If being loved is your goal, you will fail to achieve it. The only way to be assured of being loved is to be a person worthy of love, and you cannot be a person worthy of love when your primary goal in life is to be passively loved."

I started to see the same trend in some of my friends and close acquaintances who were having a hard time keeping long-term relationships, going through a divorce, or wondering why they hadn't found a compatible spouse. Most of them simply did not love themselves, and they were hoping and praying that another person was going to solve it.

What's sad is that loving yourself is probably the most overlooked form of love, but it is critical to finding happiness in your life. It seems a bit ironic that such an essential happiness component gets so little attention, but the majority of the self-help books I read focused more on loving others and having the right attitude.

But there were a few authors that really nailed it such as M. Scott Peck, Eckhart Tolle, and Kamal Ravikant. Here is what else M. Scott Peck said about loving yourself in **The Road Less Traveled**:

> "Love was defined as "the will to extend one's self for the purpose of nurturing one's own or another's spiritual growth." When we grow, it is because we are working at it, and we are working at it because we love ourselves. It is through love that we elevate ourselves. And it is through our love for others that we assist others to elevate themselves. Love, the extension of the self, is the very act of evolution. It is evolution in progress. The evolutionary force, present in all of life, manifests itself in mankind as human love. Among humanity love is the miraculous force that defies the natural law of entropy."

Powerful stuff.

And it makes sense when you step back and think about it. How can we grow as individuals or as a society if we don't love ourselves? How we can love others if we don't love ourselves? And how can any of us blindly believe that by simply finding or marrying another person it will make us happy if we don't love ourselves? Can we truly feel loved if we don't believe we're worthy of it? Of course not. Yet, so many people go around in life proclaiming to their best friends that they would be happy if they could just find that "right person." Wrong!

Here's another powerful quote on love from **The Prophet**, by Kahlil Gibran. Notice his emphasis on giving each other space (aka loving each other while at the same time loving yourself):

> *"Let there be spaces in your togetherness, and let the winds of the heavens dance between you. Love one another but make not a bond of love: Let it rather be a moving sea between the shores of your souls. Fill each other's cup but drink not from one cup. Give one another of your bread but eat not from the same loaf. Sing and dance together and be joyous, but let each one of you be alone, Even as the strings of a lute are alone though they quiver with the same music. Give your hearts, but not into each other's keeping. For only the hand of Life can contain your hearts. And stand together, yet not too near together: For the pillars of the temple stand apart, and the oak tree and the cypress grow not in each other's shadow."*

Eckhart Tolle said this about the myth of finding the right person in conjunction with loving yourself in his book, **The Power Of Now**. *"Is it not true that you need to have a good relationship with yourself and love yourself before you can have a fulfilling relationship with another person? Yes. If you cannot be at ease with yourself when you are alone, you will seek a relationship to cover up your unease. You can be sure that the unease will then reappear in some other form within the relationship, and you will probably hold your partner responsible for it."*

Yet, most of us (including me) do the following two things when it comes to our relationships and loving ourselves:

1. When we don't love ourselves, we have a tendency to think someone else (like a spouse or partner) can fix the problem
2. On the other end of the spectrum, when we have a fight, issue, or argument with our spouse or partner we have a tendency to blame and accuse them (not us) as being the problem

Eckhart Tolle had this to say about this false thinking in **The Power Of Now**:

> *"The greatest catalyst for change in a relationship is complete acceptance of your partner as he or she is, without needing to judge or change them in any way. That immediately takes you beyond ego. All mind games and all addictive clinging are then over. There are no more victims and no more perpetrators anymore, no accuser and no accused."*

And this is the exact same theme that popped up time and time again in Jason Fischer's book, **The Two Truths About Love**. Jason made it abundantly clear that the only way to have a successful (and long-lasting) relationship is to spend more time focusing on yourself and stop trying to change or alter your partner. He refers to it throughout the book as *"giving permission"* to the other person to be themselves. Here is a great quote from his book on this:

> *"When you give others permission to be who and how they are, you show them that they are okay, just as they are. Showing others love in this extraordinary way is highly nourishing. As a result, their confidence and belief in themselves grow. Instead of judging themselves as flawed or inadequate (as others have probably done), they now begin to embrace themselves as you have embraced them, emulating the permission you have given."*

Try it out yourself in your own relationships. It works wonders compared to trying to change the other person or trying to force them to see things your way. Just love yourself and grant others to love themselves as they are.

One of my other favorite quotes on loving yourself came from Kamal Ravikant. His novel, **Rebirth**, (which is an amazing tale based on his real-life pilgrimage across Spain), contained this conversation with a woman he met on the pilgrimage:

> *"Most of my life, she said, "I was my worst enemy. Then cancer gave me a gift in the form of a question. It might be too simple for you."*
> *She stopped and chuckled.*
> *"Would you like to hear it?*
>
> *"Very much."*
>
> *"Here: **If I loved myself, would I do this?**"*
>
> *"You're right," I said. "That is simple."*
>
> *"I did not choose friends anymore for their status. I started to choose friends who made me happy. Everything I did, from eating and drinking to where I live, I only did it if it was a 'yes'."*

Imagine if you and I lived like that every day? If we only pursued things that were a "yes" to the question, *If I loved myself, would I do this?* I can only assume we would be significantly happier in everything we do.

Finally, Kamal really hits the nail on the head with the power of loving yourself in his book, ***Love Yourself Like Your Life Depends On It***, with this quote:

"Love is an emotion, love is a feeling, love is a way of being. That spring in the step, that smile, that openness, can't it simply come from loving ourselves? That stops me. Of course. Here we are, thinking that one needs to be in love with another to shine, to feel free and shout from the rooftops, but the most important person, the most important relationship we'll ever have is waiting, is craving to be loved truly and deeply. You."

Let me repeat, if you can't unconditionally love yourself, then you can't love someone else the way God intended you to love.

Kamal goes on to say, *"When we love ourselves, we naturally shine, we are naturally beautiful. And that draws others to us. Before we know it, they're loving us and it's up to us to choose who to share our love with. Beautiful irony. Fall in love with yourself. Let your love express itself and the world will beat a path to your door to fall in love with you."*

"As you love yourself, life loves you back."

Love
Summary/Action Steps

THE WORD "LOVE" appears anywhere from 310 to 538 times in the **Bible** (depending on which version you reference). But regardless if you read the King James Version or the New International Version, one thing is for certain; love is critical for you to be happy and fulfilled.

I bring up the **Holy Bible** because there is a man in the **Bible** named **Jesus** that serves as one of the best examples of *love* ever born.

Regardless if you are a believer in Jesus Christ as the Savior or not, there is plenty of evidence to prove he was filled with love. I've yet to meet anyone from any religious background who doesn't agree that the world would be a better place if everyone loved and forgave like Jesus. I mean, can you imagine having twelve of your best friends turn on you when you needed them most (and one completely abandon and deny he knew you three times), all while you are being forced to carry your own cross to your own crucifixion? To make matters worse, countless people spit on you, mock you, and torture you, yet you have the will to say, *"Father forgive them, for they know not what they are doing?"*

Say what?! For most of us, forgiving the same people who are literally trying to kill you would be an almost unthinkable feat. Are you filled with that kind of love and forgiving power? I know I certainly struggle to love my enemies as much as Jesus did.

Here's a hard-hitting love quote from the Bible that I reference anytime I'm having trouble forgiving others:

> *"But if you love those who love you, what credit is that to you? For even sinners love those who love them. And if you do good to those who do good to you, what credit is that to you? For even sinners do the same... But love your enemies, do good, and lend, hoping for nothing in return; and your reward will be great, and you will be sons of the Most High. For he is kind to the unthankful and evil. Therefore be merciful, just as your Father is merciful"*

> (LUKE 6:32-36)

Powerful words. Love thy enemies.

One of my favorite podcast episodes was when Mike Dillard (from the **Self Made Man** podcast) interviewed Mike Koenigs. The interview was titled, *"What To Do When Facing Death,"* as Mike Koenigs had recently survived a severe battle with cancer. In the interview he discusses how spending many months on his deathbed in the hospital made him reflect on what is really important.

During the interview Mike refers to his cancer as *"a gift"* because it finally taught him *"how to forgive, how to love, and how to get in a deep state of gratitude."* And because of "the gift of cancer," Mike has never been happier or more fulfilled in life.

He goes on to say that *"no matter what your interpretation of The Way, The Truth, and The Life is, Jesus Christ's life is a model, an instructional blueprint for how to think, how to behave, how to treat other people, how to treat yourself, and how to feel… the Jesus Christ myth, story, or the full-on man who was the Son of God, regardless of how you see him, is a roadmap to total salvation, peace, and forgiveness."*

So what's the moral of the story and how does it relate to this chapter? Mirror and model your life after Jesus in the following five ways and you will begin to move one step closer to fulfillment:

- *Love* like Jesus
- *Forgive* like Jesus
- *Understand* like Jesus
- *Lead* like Jesus
- Have *Patience* like Jesus

One last powerful line of scripture concerning love:

> *"God is love, and he who abides in love abides in God, and God in him."*

> (1 JOHN 4:16)

THE THREE FORMS OF LOVE

I hope I made it abundantly clear that fulfillment comes when all three "love buckets" are being filled simultaneously. To ignore one (and certainly two) of the buckets will leave you feeling empty inside. It is the blend of family love, community love, and loving oneself that brings true happiness.

Here is one final quote from M. Scott Peck in his book, **The Road Less Traveled**, regarding the importance of all three forms of love:

> *"The ultimate goal of life remains the spiritual growth of the individual, the solitary journey to peaks that can be climbed only alone. Significant*

journeys cannot be accomplished without the nurture provided by a successful marriage or a successful society. Marriage and society exist for the basic purpose of nurturing such individual journeys."

YOUR LOVE ACTION STEPS

1. First and foremost, start loving yourself. We've spent a lot of time in earlier chapters talking about how happiness is a choice you have to make. Guess what? So is love. You can either choose to love yourself or not. You don't need any material thing to make it happen except a conscious decision to love yourself.

2. Next, analyze your relationships. Are they healthy? Are the people around you lifting you up or bringing you down? Write down your closest friends and decide who you really need to invest more time with and who you need to distance yourself from. Your happiness can be jeopardized by hanging around unhappy and negative people (even family). Always give them a chance and encourage them to read books like this, but if they never change, then spend less time with them and build healthier relationships.

3. If you are married, I highly suggest picking one day a week that is your "SACRED" night, when the two of you catch up and hang out with no distractions. It is way too easy to get caught up in life and wake up one day realizing you haven't had a date night with your spouse in months. Not good! My wife and I recently agreed that Friday nights were our sacred night. No exceptions. We treat it like a pastor would treat showing up to work on Sunday. No excuses!

4. Next, start working on becoming a better listener. As you read above, the ultimate form of LOVE is giving someone your full ATTENTION. So give your loved ones your time (while being fully engaged), and give them your full attention.

5. Then spend some time really thinking about your legacy. What do you want to leave behind when you die? Do kids fit in the picture?

Does a spouse? What can you start doing today to improve your chances of leaving a lasting and memorable legacy?

6. Finally, open up a new checking account and start putting 10% of your take-home income in it every month.

DAILY, WEEKLY, AND MONTHLY ACTION STEPS

Daily:

- Wake up and smile while getting ready and in the shower. Mike Dillard, a highly successful entrepreneur and investor, says that just by purposely smiling while he takes a shower every morning he has found himself to be happier and friendlier to people the rest of the day (and others around him have noticed his happiness too).
- Make a point to smile and say hello to a complete stranger every day. Wish a complete stranger happiness.
- Tell your immediate family members you love them and spend time listening to them. You never know when one of them (or you) will not be around again.
- Model your life (in terms of love, forgiveness, and patience) after Jesus.

Weekly:

- Make a point to meet one new person every week. Even if it's just a simple conversation, handshake, and asking their name. It can be a neighbor, someone at the gym, your kid's school, etc. Some of my best friends in Tampa started from a simple hello when I could have just as easily said nothing and never met them.
- Make a point to tell your extended family members you love them.

Monthly:

- For the next twelve months, write down twelve of your closest friends or family members that you have either lost touch with or just can't find the time to call. Write down a specific date and time that you are going to call them and surprise them that day. Even if you have to leave a voicemail, it will feel amazing to reconnect with these people.
- Give 10% of your take-home income away. No exceptions.

Finally, have FUN!

Research shows that people who regularly have fun are twenty times more likely to feel happy compared to those who stick with the same old daily routines. Break out of your routine. Don't get caught doing the exact same boring thing over and over again Monday through Friday. Life is too short! Mix it up. Take some chances. Go try something new and exciting and meet some new friends along the way.

P.S. – Don't ever scalp boy band concert tickets. It won't make you any happier...

Cornerstone #4

ACTION

Action

Overview

AUTHOR OF *LIVE **Your Truth***, Kamal Ravikant, was having dinner with his friend Joanna. Though she was only in her early thirties, Joanna was a national champion rower, had risen up in the ranks of the FBI, had trained countless members of the Iraqi and Afghan police force, and was now CEO of a big company in Silicon Valley. "What shaped you into the person you are today?" Kamal wanted to know. "And how do you manage to do so much, while looking like you're having the best time in the world?"

She responded with, "After I came out of the coma, everything changed. Anything I want for my life happens... it just comes to me."

When Joanna was twenty-four years old she suffered a severe heart attack. She doesn't remember anything except what the doctors told her after she woke up a month later: that she flat-lined, was resuscitated, she remained in a coma for quite some time, and that she was lucky to be alive.

Kamal smiled at his friend's answer and pressed further. "I don't want to have to die to figure out your secret. What changed? You've got to tell me!"

Joanna leaned forward, looked straight into Kamal's eyes, and said in a soft voice, "You're going to think I am crazy… **but what if this is heaven?**"

Silence.

She continued, "Kamal, I died in the hospital that day. I know that for sure. But what I can't prove is that I came back to life. How can I know that this isn't the other side? No one has been able to tell me that it isn't. So because of that, I wake up every day believing this is heaven. And because this is heaven, I can have, be, and do anything I want—that is how I have lived life ever since."

Wow! Talk about completely altering your view on life. Joanna used her misfortune to completely change the way she sees herself and the world. No wonder she has been able to accomplish so much and get anything she wants.

How many of us go to sleep dreading the sound of the alarm clock, going to work, and facing the day? How many of us come home complaining? Joanna would probably agree with *Zig Ziglar's* response to the lady who was complaining to him about having a "bad day." Here's what Zig replied back to the negative lady groveling about her day: *"That's nothing. You want to experience a bad day, try skipping just one and let me know how that works for you."*

After pondering Kamal's story about his friend Joanna, and what I had read in other books regarding attitude and perspective, it hit me.

IN ORDER TO ACHIEVE LONG-TERM HAPPINESS AND FULFILLMENT YOU MUST:

- **Change the way you see the world.**
- **Change the way you see yourself.**

What Joanna and so many other fulfilled people have figured out is that to be happy, you must fully believe that life is happening FOR you, not TO you. Fulfilled people live every day knowing that everything happens for a reason. They make the best out of everything (good and bad), and they firmly believe that everything that occurs in life will eventually benefit them. They don't blame the world for things that go wrong; they embrace them and learn from them. They don't react to problems; they respond to them. They don't let bad times or suffering destroy them; they use these experiences to excel and reach new heights.

This final cornerstone is all about ***perspective, attitude, and taking action*** to create the happy and fulfilled life you want.

13

Say The "F-Word" More!

I WOKE UP that morning and pulled my pillow over my head. I didn't want to come out from under my covers and start the day. One more snooze wouldn't hurt anybody. Especially when you consider that I was unemployed, broke, low on self-esteem, and even lower on happiness.

As I rolled around in bed that morning, I couldn't help but wonder how life had changed so drastically for me in just a few months. About a year ago I was living in Australia and New Zealand having the best time of my life with some amazing people on a study abroad trip. Less than six months ago I was back in the states enjoying my senior year at Georgia Tech where I considered myself a BMOC (big man on campus). And just three months ago I was up on stage at Georgia Tech graduating with highest honors.

Now here I was sleeping in until nine am, living with my parents in Winter Haven, Florida, and jobless with little to no solid prospects. All of my closest friends were employed, so there wasn't much to do during the day. I felt like a failure, and to make matters worse, I was suffering from constant panic attacks. Talk about going from Cloud Nine to the pavement in a short period!

If you've ever experienced being unemployed for any amount of time, you know that it is not a pleasant experience. Every day that goes by without a job results in more stress, more anxiety, and more bills that get tougher to pay. But the worse part is when all of your friends and loved ones keep asking, "Any luck on the job front?"

"NO!" I wanted to yell at them after being asked for the second, third, and fourteenth time. "If I get a job, trust me, you will hear about it. Stop asking!"

So here I was going on three months without a job, and I couldn't see an end in sight. I had a few interviews with banks, and a couple lunch meetings with family friends in high positions (hoping to get my foot in the door), but no one was hiring me. A few prospects even rejected me for being overqualified. They said they knew any training they invested in me would be a waste: "You would be gone the second something better came along." They were probably right.

But I had reached the point where I didn't care. I would do anything to get the monkey off my back and finally stop the, "Any luck on the job front, Joe?" questioning.

I started applying for just about any job you can imagine. I was dead set on getting a job, and I didn't care about the pay, the hours, or anything else for that matter. I just wanted a paycheck and a little respect.

With no luck on the job front (the tech bubble had recently imploded and it was a less than ideal time for a new grad to be searching for their dream job—or any job for that matter), I decided to apply to be a substitute teacher. It didn't pay well, and it certainly wasn't full-time, but I felt like I was at a dead end.

After filling out some paperwork, I waited for my first substitute teacher call. And waited. And waited. Did any of these teachers ever get sick? Did they not get my application? I waited and waited. Still, the phone never rang. Not once. After enough time had passed I could no longer hide from the cold, hard truth; I was a substitute-teaching reject. Rock bottom never felt so hard.

I was borderline depressed. I felt like a failure. I was beginning to think I would be living with my parents indefinitely. I could no longer imagine having the successful career that seemed within reach just months prior. I had repeatedly lowered the bar on my expectations—I would have taken just about anything—and still nothing. So what did I do next?

I prayed. And I prayed *hard*. I prayed for God to open up the right job at the right time. I prayed that the right door would open up and that I would be smart enough to know I should run through it. And I prayed that I could start thinking BIG again and not be stuck settling for any lame job. I slowly began convincing myself that I would find it.

You'll never believe what happened just a week after changing my mindset with prayer and a little faith. While visiting a girl I was dating in Atlanta (who somehow didn't give up on me even though I was unemployed and living with my parents seven hours away), I got a call on my cell phone from a recruiter. He had seen my resume on the Georgia Tech job website and wanted to know if I was still on the hunt.

"Um, yes, you could say that."

He told me I might be a fit for an entry-level sales position with a young, fast-growing financial marketing company in Atlanta. He said that the president of the company wanted to interview me on Monday and asked if I was available.

I was supposed to fly out the next day and didn't have much money to change flights, but I knew I needed to go to this interview. So I told him yes, paid Delta to push my flight to Tuesday, borrowed my buddy Chris' suit, borrowed my girlfriend's car, and headed up to Woodstock, Georgia to interview with the president of the company. After a fantastic two-hour interview, I flew back to Florida where I received a call that the job was mine if I wanted it.

The salary was a bit lower than that which the average Georgia Tech grad was receiving, but I had the ability to earn monthly commissions based on my performance. I stayed there a full nine years (and ended up raking in seven figures throughout my nine years there) before moving on to start my first company. And through it all, I got in the habit of saying the "F-word."

FAILURE.

Here's a word that pops up in practically every personal development, business, and happiness book that I read. It is a word that has helped shape some of the wisest and most successful leaders in the world. And yet we avoid it like the plague. Let's discuss why this word is so critical to understand, and why it should be used and talked about more often to both kids and adults.

All throughout life I was told the way to AVOID being a failure was to study hard, get good grades, stay out of trouble, go to a good college, get a good job, and work my way up the ladder. I had stuck to that plan my whole life. I graduated near the top of my class in high school and then graduated with highest honors with two minors at Georgia Tech. I had a great background, some top-notch schooling, and yet not once had I taken a course or had a lecture on the importance of failure (and how to handle it). In fact, over the course of my whole education, I had never learned that failure, disappointments, and setbacks are inevitable.

You will hit bumps in the road. You will have bad days, bad weeks, and even bad months. You will lose loved ones. You will lose friends. You will lose money. You will lose countless times throughout the span of your life, and it will be your ability to accept, conquer, and overcome those losses and failures that will determine your happiness. As Ryan Holiday points out in **The Obstacle Is The Way**, *"it is your ability to conquer and learn from obstacles and failures that make you stronger in life."*

Our schools and even most families avoid talking about this word "failure." We treat it like it is taboo today. We give losing teams trophies so their feelings won't get hurt, we try to trick young kids into believing they won when they lost, and we'll do everything we can to avoid talking about failing. What a disservice to our children. Failure is critical to achieving success and happiness!

I firmly believe that if you never fail, then you aren't trying hard enough. How can you be prepared to deal with a huge loss (like the loss of a loved one, loss of a job, etc.) if you can't handle losing a baseball or soccer game?

It was **Benjamin Franklin** who said, *"Those things that hurt, instruct."* Book after book that I read from highly successful people all said similar things. You grow and gain wisdom from your mistakes, problems, and obstacles.

One of my favorite quotes comes from **Fred Smith** who says, *"It's impossible to climb a smooth mountain."* In other words, if there aren't a few bumps and rocks along the way, it's impossible to reach the peak!

The mountain metaphors don't stop there. In reminding his readers to appreciate and embrace all of the bumps in the road to finding fulfillment, Tal Ben-Shahar, Harvard professor and author of **Happier** said, *"Attaining lasting happiness requires that we enjoy the journey on our way toward a destination we deem valuable. Happiness is not about making it to the peak of the mountain nor is it about climbing aimlessly around the mountain; happiness is the experience of climbing toward the peak."* I couldn't agree more!

Let's look at it another way. If you've never had a rough day, how will you ever know if you are happy? If you've never been sick a day in your life, how can you tell if you're feeling great? It might sound weird, but how would you know what success or happiness feels like if you've never experienced the opposite?

So why is it that the word "failure" has such a negative connotation in schools and within families when every successful person was an EPIC FAILURE at one point (or many) in their lives? In fact, I am pretty certain that there wasn't a single successful person whom I read about or met personally in my mastermind group who didn't go through some tough times, experience crushing rejection(s), or have a pivotal moment in life where a letdown or an obstacle forged who they became.

Just look at **Walt Disney**. Did you know that he filed for bankruptcy multiple times, was days from being homeless (he lived like a homeless person on numerous occasions), and was laughed at by most of Hollywood for years before making it big?

Did you know that Thomas Edison failed approximately 10,000 times before building a light bulb that worked? When asked why he kept going after failing so many times, Edison famously said, *"I haven't failed. I've just found 10,000 ways that won't work."* This is from a guy who watched his entire office building burn down!

When most people would have been ready to throw in the towel and find a new job, Leonard DeGraaf tells us in his book, *Edison*, that the famous inventor said the following as he watched his entire life's work burn up in flames:

"In a childlike voice, Edison told his 24-year old son, "Go get your mother and all her friends. They'll never see a fire like this again. When his son

Charles objected, Edison said, "It's all right. We've just got rid of a lot of rubbish."

Talk about having the right mindset when it comes to accepting failure!

Billionaire **Mark Cuban** was unemployed, overweight, and living on his friend's couch. And yet, he continued to "fail forward" until he sold his business for more money than most of us will ever see in a lifetime.

"Failing Forward" is something that everyone should employ in their lives, and I highly encourage you to read the book of the same title *Failing Forward* by John Maxwell. John nails it when he says, *"When it comes right down to it, I know of only one factor that separates those who consistently shine from those who don't: The difference between average people and achieving people is their perception of and response to failure. Nothing else has the same kind of impact on people's ability to achieve and to accomplish whatever their minds and hearts desire."*

Another analogy that has always stuck with me comes from Maxwell Maltz's, *The New Psycho-Cybernetics*, in which he said, *"A guided torpedo arrives at its target literally by making a series of mistakes* (in most cases thousands of mistakes) *and continually correcting its course. You cannot correct your course if you are standing still. You cannot change or correct nothing."*

Ryan Holiday has a similar message about the value of seeing failure of as course-correction in *The Obstacle Is The Way*: *"Failure shows us the way by showing us what isn't the way."* There are lessons to be learned in our setbacks. I'm sure basketball coach, Rick Pitino, would agree with Ryan's message. He saw the educational value of experiencing failure with his quote: *"Failure is good. It's fertilizer. Everything I've learned about coaching I've learned from making mistakes."* The moral of the story is that if you don't fail, you don't gain experience. And if you don't gain experience then you don't grow. If you aren't growing, then you are dying.

Disney, Edison, Cuban, and all of the world's most successful and fulfilled people would all likely tell you that failure is one of the keys to opening up new doors to happiness. So when you do fail at something—and you will—embrace it and learn from it. Know that with every failure you are one step closer to excellence.

The Power Of Broke by Daymond John was the book that changed a lot of things about my current lifestyle brands called Salt Strong and Fish Strong. When I read the book our company was pretty low on cash, and we weren't 100% sure what we stood for. But after reading all of the amazing success stories from Daymond's book (which is filled with true stories of people who went from being broke to rich by failing forward and pursuing their passion in life), we did a complete 180 with our business. I now encourage my employees and business partner to "double your failure rate." That's right; I want my employees (and myself) willing to take risks, learn from their mistakes, and figure out how to correct them moving forward. I believe it will make us stronger as individuals and as a company. If you aren't failing, then you aren't growing.

A powerful quote from *The Power Of Broke* came from Daymond's chapter on Mark Burnett (producer of Survivor, Apprentice, The Voice, and Shark Tank). Here is what Mark said was key in making big things happen:

> *"My motivator was the fear of looking back and regretting that I didn't take one of these risks my mom was always talking about. My pain was the fear of future regret, so I didn't care so much whether things worked out. I only cared that I took the action and tried. Really, if you have hope, in anything you do, you can make it."*

He ends the chapter with Mark's favorite biblical passages from the book of Romans: *"Suffering produces perseverance: perseverance, character: and character, hope."*

Walt Disney struck a similar chord when he said, *"All the adversity I've had in my life, all my troubles and obstacles, have strengthened me. You may not realize it when it happens, but a kick in the teeth may be the best thing in the world for you."*

Accept failure in your life. Learn from it, and let it make you stronger. Your happiness depends on it.

14

How This Kid In A Wheelchair
Proves Happiness Is A Choice

I WAS ONLY seven years old, but I can still see the room. I can still picture the mustard-green rocking chair my mom was sitting in as she held my infant brother Daniel in her arms. I can still see the tears running down her face.

I was too young to understand what was going on, but I knew something wasn't right. We all knew that Daniel, my youngest brother, was a special kid early on. But I don't think anyone, least of all my parents, expected the news we got that day.

"Cerebral Palsy," the doctors told them. They didn't know how bad it was—Daniel was still too young. "But he will likely be in a wheelchair for some or all of his life."

Learning that their son had a physical disability came as a hard blow after nine months of pregnancy and a stressful birth, but my parents took the news well. Yes, there were some tears shed over the diagnosis, but they weren't unhappy about Daniel's life. They certainly didn't love him any less. "We knew that God had blessed us with this sweet boy," my mom told me years later, "and we trusted that Daniel was born with CP for a reason. Time will tell us why."

At the age when most babies are starting to take their first steps progressing from crawling to walking, Daniel still lay stuck to the floor. He had a forceful grip with his arms, but his legs, tongue, and pretty much every other muscle in his body weren't functioning and maturing like a typical toddler. I was still too young to know what cerebral palsy meant, but my parents succinctly put it this way: "Daniel is an incredibly special kid that thinks, hears, and understands just like you and me. He just has much weaker muscles in all parts of his body." Put that way, it made plenty of sense to me.

As it became clearer and clearer that our brother Daniel was not going to be able to walk, he started going through some pretty intense physical therapy. I still remember the long drives to Lakeland and Tampa from Winter Haven with Daniel and my mom. I was young but still smart enough to realize that many of these exercises were extremely painful for Daniel. They were pushing his weak muscles and joints to places they had never been before, and many days he would be in tears. Still, he almost always had a big smile ready to flash at any given moment.

Eventually, Daniel (aka "Dan the Man") got his first wheelchair. He didn't have the upper body strength to push himself, so he depended on us to take him everywhere. My other brother Luke and I thought it was pretty cool to wheel him around and make him laugh. Dan was always happy with that big, contagious smile for which he was becoming known.

Many people don't know this, but when you spend the majority of your early years slumped over in a wheelchair with little muscle strength to keep you up, your body still continues to grow even if you aren't upright. As your arms, legs, fingers, spine, and everything else continue to grow while in unnatural positions, your body slowly becomes distorted. My incredibly strong and supportive parents did everything in their power to help "straighten" Daniel out. He underwent more surgeries and procedures than I can recall. From multiple leg braces trying to straighten out his legs to a back surgery that involved more 'breaking' than anything else, Daniel has been cut up, pulled apart, and stretched out more times than he cares to remember.

But somehow Daniel managed to stay strong and come out of each ordeal with a smile. The amount of pain he has had to suffer through before the age of thirty is something you wouldn't wish upon your worst enemy. Yet every day Daniel woke up with a smile. And never once did Daniel feel sorry for himself.

As you can imagine, Daniel had a much different experience growing up than most teenagers. While most kids would fear getting picked last for sports games, Daniel never got picked at all. While my brother Luke and I played multiple sports in high school, Daniel sat on the sidelines and watched from his wheelchair. He has never been part of a sports team. He has never felt the rush of running out on a field with fans cheering or the joy of winning a game of any sort—he has never even sat in the bleachers. But Daniel continues to find joy every day.

As if this weren't tough enough, Daniel also can't talk. You see, with advanced cerebral palsy like his, ALL of his muscles are weaker than normal including his tongue. I can still recall the excitement in our house when Daniel got his first Dynavox voice synthesized computer. This box would allow Daniel to hit pre-programmed buttons that would talk for him. For instance, he would hit one button that would say, "I have to go to the bathroom," while another button would say (in a funny, robot-like voice), "My name is Dan the Man Simonds. What is your name?"

One of the best lines he ever programmed was a little bit later in life when Luke and I were in college. Daniel would go up to a cute girl, flash his big smile, and then hit a button that would say, "Are you tired?"

The girl, usually a bit dumbfounded as to why this little guy in a wheelchair was asking her if she is tired, would always say, "No… why do you ask?"

Then Daniel would excitedly hit the next button on his computer, which would say, "Because you've been running through my mind. All. Day. Long."

It was pretty epic, and there wasn't a single girl that didn't think it was funny. Most of them would even give their phone number to Dan the Man thinking a little kid that can't talk would never call them. Boy were they wrong!

But it wasn't all fun and games with the three of us brothers. It's sad to look back and have to write about it, but almost all young teenage boys go through this stage. I'm referring to the stage where your family (especially your mom and dad) embarrass you, and you are trying everything in your power to look cool, to make sure your friends know you are cool, and that all of the girls know you are cool. Any embarrassing moment feels magnified by ten thousand percent, and you'll do anything to avoid looking dumb. I'm talking about that 13-16-year-old range. And if you thought it was embarrassing for a 15-year-old boy to be seen with his mom hanging around him everywhere he goes, you can't even imagine how embarrassing it was to have a kid in a wheelchair follow you everywhere.

You see, my brother not only stood out like a sore thumb in his motorized wheelchair, but he was always drooling, and in my mind, he was doing nothing but hurting my cool points with the girls. People didn't know how to act or what to say to him back then, and sadly, just like many people in wheelchairs, I could clearly see people were avoiding Dan. This also meant that they were avoiding me when he was next to me.

Numerous times I remember being a punk teenager and yelling at my mom that I didn't want to have Daniel tag along with me at an event.

I thought he would embarrass me and make me look bad. Little did I know that I was the one looking like a fool. As a teenager, I did my fair share of dumb, senseless, and even mean things. But there isn't anything I regret more than how I treated my brother for those couple of years. The crazy part is that Daniel never got angry with me about it... not one time. Even though he was six years younger, it was like he understood. He was willing to forgive me at the drop of a hat. While I tried to avoid him, Daniel loved me unconditionally and made sure that I knew it. I still think he might be Superman disguised in the body of a kid in a wheelchair.

HAPPINESS IS A CHOICE

Neil Pasricha nailed it in his book, **The Happiness Equation**, when he said:

"Happy people don't have the best of everything. They make the best of everything. Be happy first."

And as Scott Adams says in **How To Fail At Almost Everything And Still Win Big**, *"your attitude affects everything you do in your quest for success and happiness."* I couldn't agree more.

My brother Daniel is happy. He carries a smile with him all day long. He is full of energy that never stops. It's almost as though he doesn't realize he is disabled. His handicap mysteriously brought my parents and our entire family closer together, and he is certainly part of the glue that has kept us so close.

Dan the Man lives with more energy, more affection, and more happiness than most people I know. People who have everything that he lacks. Most of us will never have to experience what it's like to wake up every morning and wait patiently wait for someone to lift us out of bed into our wheelchair. Most of us will never have to wait for someone to help us get dressed and fed. Most of us will never have to wear a diaper our entire lives. Most of us will never spend our whole life without ever saying a complete sentence. But not Daniel. That is his life every single day. And he is *incredibly grateful* for it.

While we whine when our Wi-Fi is slow, or complain that life isn't fair when we don't get our way, and commiserate with co-workers about how much we dislike our jobs, Daniel is thanking God for another amazing day on Earth. He believes he is lucky to be alive and lives every day in the moment. When things don't go his way, he still smiles. His example is one that I try to follow, and his perspective is one I try to keep. As far as role models go, it doesn't get much better than Dan the Man.

Mike Hernacki nails it in his book, ***The Ultimate Secret To Getting Everything You Want,*** with this quote:

> *"What can you do to achieve happiness? Well, if you're unhappy about being poor, you could makes lots of money. Would that work? I'm afraid not. Money is nice to have, but it's no guarantee of happiness. If it were, all rich people would be happy, and we know that this simply isn't so.*
>
> *Suppose you're unhappy being single. Well, you could get married, but as the divorce statistics show, plenty of married people are quite miserable.*
>
> *The point is, there's nothing you can do to become happy. You can only be it."*

HAPPINESS IS A CHOICE

If you believe you are happy, you will be. Happiness isn't something that happens to you. It's an attitude. It's a perspective. Happiness is your attitude on life and how you see the world. Happiness is something you can choose to be. So many people choose (whether consciously or through habit) to focus on all of the negatives instead of the positives. Guess where they fall on the happiness spectrum?

Guess what they can do to change it?

Author Normal Vincent Peale has an entire chapter dedicated to this idea in his book, *The Power Of Positive Thinking*, called "How To Create Your Own Happiness." In that chapter, he tells the story of a TV celebrity who had an older man on his show. The older man had an incredibly unique happiness about him. Here is the story from the book:

> *"Finally the celebrity asked the old man why he was so happy. "You must have a wonderful secret of happiness," he suggested. "No," replied the old man, "I haven't any great secret. It's just as plain as the nose on your face. When I get up in the morning, I have two choices - either be happy or be unhappy, and what do you think I do? I just choose to be happy, and that's all there is to it."*

Neil Pasricha describes research from a California psychology professor named Sonja Lyubomirsky in his book, *The Happiness Equation,* which revealed the following: "*10% of our happiness is what happens to us. 90% of our happiness is based on how we see the world.*"

90%!! The bulk of our happiness comes from making the choice to see it! There is a story that I love in the book, *Life Is Good*, in which Bert and John Jacobs talked about how they *learned* optimism while they were kids. Their mom, Joan (a big inspiration for the Life is Good brand), would ask the kids every single night at dinner, *"Tell me something good that happened today."*

One by one the kids would go around the table talking about the good things that happened that day. In their book, Bert and John said this about their mother and her years of making them start every dinner with positive stories:

> *"Eventually we became conscious of the fact that joy doesn't come from your circumstances. It comes from your disposition. This deep-rooted belief would only grow stronger as we became adults. Even at our worst moments, we've always had the tools that we needed to survive because of Mom. She showed us that optimism is a courageous choice you can make every day, especially in the face of adversity."*

The idea is so simple. **Choose to see happiness**.

It's an amazing thing to realize that you have control over whether you are happy or not. It's even crazier to think that the choice to be happy is as simple as deciding to look for the good things in your day or to find the "silver lining" in a tough situation. As Matthieu Ricard says in **Happiness**, *"Happiness is also a way of interpreting the world, since while it may be difficult to change the world, it is always possible to change the way we look at it."* There is so much you can achieve by being willing to change your perspective— especially in the face of hardship.

Ryan Holiday talks about this idea in **The Obstacle Is The Way**. He went out of his way to prove that "obstacles" (aka roadblocks, bad times, rock bottom) are the key to happiness if we take the time to overcome them and learn from them. Here are the things he suggests we remember in the face of adversity:

> *"In every situation we can:*
>
> *Always prepare ourselves for more difficult times.*
> *Always accept what we're unable to change.*
> *Always manage our expectations.*

Always persevere.
Always learn to love our fate and what happens to us.
Always protect our inner self, retreat into ourselves.
Always submit to a greater, larger cause.
Always remind ourselves of our own mortality.

There is an entire list of choices available to us in even the worst of times, a whole collection of things that are within our control. I would also add another item to it: we can choose to see the "silver lining" in any scenario.

Along these same lines, Matthieu Ricard reminds us that, "*The next step after we discard our expectations and accept what happens to us, after understanding that certain things - particularly bad things - are outside our control, is this: loving whatever happens to us and facing it with unfailing cheerfulness.*" In other words, we can choose to be happy anyway.

Neurologist and psychiatrist Dr. Viktor Frankl said in **Man's Search For Meaning**, "*Everything can be taken from a man but one thing: the last of the human freedoms - to choose one's attitude in any given set of circumstances, to choose one's own way.*"

And **Zig Ziglar** said, "*It's not what happens to you that determines how far you will go in life; it is how you handle what happens to you.*"

My brother Daniel can't talk, walk, drive a car, or do most things that the vast majority of Americans take for granted. He doesn't dwell on these facts. He doesn't focus on the things he can't do, and he certainly doesn't focus on that fact that his arms and legs don't work or that he cannot speak. Instead, he smiles all the time, he tells corny jokes, and makes sure we know how much he loves us.

Dan the Man chooses to be happy. And so he is.

You can choose whether or not to be happy. Dan the man is living proof.

Happiness is a CHOICE.

15

You'll Never Be Truly Fulfilled
Without This In Your Life

I STARED OUT the window from my work cubicle into the parking lot. The woman I'd just been speaking with left after having just given me the worst news of my life. *Cancer*. I thought my life was over as I knew it. I couldn't concentrate on work, and I left early that afternoon feeling depressed.

Two weeks earlier I was heading back home from a business trip. We were still sitting at the gate, and although I was worn out and wanted nothing more than to sleep, the guy sitting next to me had other plans. After hearing about his trip, his kids, and whatever else he was rambling about, I did the old "book trick." I dug down in my backpack on the floor, pulled out a book, and let him know that I didn't intend to chat the entire flight home.

While I was reading and waiting for the plane to finally take off, I caught the guy staring down at my right arm out of the corner of his eye. I kept reading, hoping he wasn't about to start up another conversation. About a minute later he hit me with it. "You need to get that mole on your arm checked out."

"Are you a doctor or something?" I asked somewhat sarcastically.

"Nope, but I have had some family members deal with skin cancer, so I am always looking for irregular or discolored moles. It might just be inflamed or something, but you should definitely see a dermatologist and get it looked at."

"Thank you," I replied. "I probably do need to go in and get a check-up. It has been a few years."

The next day back at work I was slammed trying to catch up, but I couldn't get what that guy told me out of my head. More specifically, I couldn't stop looking at what appeared to be an angry looking red mole on my right arm. As usual life got in the way, and I put it off for another day.

The following morning I woke up, hopped in the shower, and all I could see was the darn red mole on my arm staring back at me. So I promised myself that I would take a break from work and make an appointment to see the dermatologist.

Fortunately for me there was a dermatologist's office upstairs in the same office building where I worked. I would occasionally flirt with the nurses that worked there when I saw them in the elevator, so I decided to just walk in and see if they could fit me in. It turned out they just received a cancellation for the following day, so if I could come in at 8:30 am I could take that spot.

Just a week after the appointment, that "angry" spot on my arm was about to get a new name. *Cancer.*

"Knock, knock," said one of the nurses who worked upstairs at the dermatologist's office as she walked up to my cubicle. She quickly realized that I was on the phone and whispered, "Sorry, I'll wait right here." I gave her the standard "one more minute" with my index finger while I tried to wrap up the call.

But honestly, the only thing I could think about was why was this nurse from the dermatologist's office here in my office? My mind shot to the small sample of skin the dermatologist had removed for a biopsy a week ago. I had completely forgotten about it, but now I quickly put the pieces of the puzzle together while pretending to listen to the voice on the other end of the phone.

As the guy on the other end of the line talked, the only thing I could think about was the fact that nurses don't walk downstairs in the middle of the day to deliver good news. They could have just as easily called me if the biopsy was fine. My forehead started to bead up with sweat, and the beginning of a panic attack set in. I grabbed my big bottle of water off the desk and muted the phone while I gulped down some cold water to cool myself off. A minute later I was finally off the phone facing this nurse as she stared at me.

"Hey, how's it going?" I asked while trying to seem cool and collected.

She wasn't smiling like she normally did when I saw her in the elevator.

"Joe, I hate to come down here during business hours and interrupt, but I have some bad news that needs to be addressed quickly."

I sat there like a deer caught in the headlights waiting for her to tell me I was dying.

"Joe, the biopsy came back, and it wasn't good. You have malignant melanoma in your right arm. It appears that it could be Stage 2 cancer, and it looks pretty deep in your arm. We'll be getting you in touch with a skin cancer surgeon so we can see if it has spread."

I couldn't remember anything else she said that day. My mind was racing as I tried to figure out what all of this meant for me. All kinds of thoughts were going through my head. Would they have to amputate my arm? What if it spread to the rest of body? I can't do chemo. I would look horrible as a bald guy. This wasn't how my life was supposed to end, was it? I have too many things left to do. I am only 28 years old for crying out loud. God, why me?

The next couple of weeks were BRUTAL. The only thing worse than finding out you have cancer is having no idea how bad it is, and then being told you won't get any real answers until after you have surgery. I had multiple doctor appointments at St. Joseph's hospital in Atlanta, and never in my life have I been so scared about something.

Many of my friends came by to cheer me up as the news spread. My parents tried to distract me with small gifts, constant phone calls, and even a trip up from Florida to see me. My mom is a very religious woman, and she tried to comfort me with a prophecy of sorts. God, she said, was telling her that I would meet the girl of my dreams because of this bout with cancer.

Whatever Mom, I thought. *I'm here afraid I'm going to die from skin cancer, and you are over here talking about meeting girls.* As much as I'd normally like to focus on girls, this was the last thing on my mind at the time. Besides, who would want to date a guy who just found out he had skin cancer and might die?

While I was at St. Joseph's doing some last-minute tests before my surgery, I was trying my best to be positive and happy while feeling alone and very anxious. After flirting a bit with the nurses who were taking my blood and doing some other tests, I was finally done with my pre-checks. Back to work.

As I was walking out of the hospital, a nurse came and tapped me on the shoulder. I turned around and she had a piece of paper in her hand. She said, "Hey there. She could get in serious trouble for this, but Sandy wanted you to have her phone number. Do whatever you want with it…"

Well, let me tell you something. I walked out of that hospital feeling like I was Brad Pitt. Pa-POW! I was on fire! What cancer? A day later I called the nurse, and we set up a date to go watch an Atlanta Braves game that upcoming Friday night.

While having a great time at the Braves game with my date, I had to hit the bathroom during the seventh inning stretch. On the way back to my seat I ran into an old friend from Georgia Tech named Chi. I hadn't seen her in years, so we caught up briefly, and she introduced me to her attractive friend, who had just walked up.

Let me back up real quick. Her friend wasn't just attractive, she was stunning! Short blonde hair, piercing blue eyes, a huge smile with perfect teeth, and the ripped body of a very fit runner. I couldn't stop thinking about her as I walked back to my seat at the game.

The following day I still couldn't get my mind off this girl whom I had met on the way back from the bathroom at the Braves game. There was just one problem. I had no idea who she was or how to reach her. I didn't have Chi's number, but I remembered that my good friend Jacqui Woo was friends with her and would probably have her number.

I called up Jacqui and got the full scoop. This blonde girl was indeed single (from what Jacqui knew), and she was in town from Augusta for the weekend to celebrate Chi's birthday. They were all going to be at a bar that evening for dinner and drinks.

It was time to go on the hunt. I had to meet this girl whom I couldn't stop thinking about. Skin cancer could wait.

I convinced my friend Jason and a few others to hit up Buckhead to help me search for this girl. All I knew was that she would be somewhere in the East Andrews bar area (which has numerous bars all tied in together), and that she should be with her friend Chi and a bunch of other girls.

Numerous drinks and many hours later, I had all but given up. It was almost 1 am and I still had not seen the mysterious blonde that I had been searching for all night. I headed upstairs where a band was playing, and I went up to the top deck so I could look over the crowd and see if she happened to be down there. I stood up there drinking my vodka tonic and was just about to walk back downstairs to call it a night when I saw her out of the corner of my eye.

She was in-between the dance floor and the seated bar area in the far left corner. I saw Chi as well, so there was no mistaking that this was the right girl. I practically ran down the stairs so that I didn't miss my opportunity, and a minute later I was face to face with this rare beauty.

"Hey there, didn't I meet you last night at the Braves game?" I asked with the biggest smile my drunken mouth would allow.

She smiled. "Oh yeah, it's Jeff, right?"

Wrong name, but at least she remembered me, I thought to myself. "You're close. My name is Joe."

For the next fifteen minutes we talked about who knows what. It was as loud as can be, I had been drinking now for five hours (while looking for her), and I was just happy have finally found her. I went in for the close by telling her I had to leave, but I would love to get her number and have dinner in the near future.

Mission Accomplished. I left with her phone number and a big smile. Life was good.

Just five days after getting her number I was on my way to pick up this girl for our first date. I was as nervous as can be, and I had the air conditioning cranked down as low as possible so that I didn't have a panic attack. Of course the other thing bothering me was whether to tell her the truth about my skin cancer.

She looked stunning when I picked her up at the door. Those big blue eyes were even brighter than I had remembered, and I couldn't help but be drawn to her contagious smile. We got in my truck and headed over to a restaurant that was close to my alma mater.

On the way there I kept going back and forth in my head... should I say something about my skin cancer or just keep it to myself? She told me she was in medical school, so I decided to keep the medical conversation going and just went for it. It was like a last-minute hail mary in a football game, and I knew it. She was either going to write me off as someone who was most likely going to die (especially since she was just a year from graduating and becoming a doctor), or she was going to have sympathy for me and want to help me through it all. I was hoping for the latter.

She absolutely shocked me with her response!

After telling her about my skin cancer, the upcoming surgery, and how bad it could be, she looked over at me in silence. I was driving so I couldn't stare at her, but I looked over ever so briefly and locked eyes before looking back ahead at the road.

She said, "Joe, you won't believe this but I actually had melanoma myself a few years ago. I haven't really told anyone except my family, and it is amazing to finally connect with someone who understands."

Holy Smokes! I thought to myself. *This girl is a gift from God.*

The rest of the date went amazingly well. We chatted and got to know each other for over four hours, and I dropped her off without even going in for the kiss. I wanted to make sure I had another date with this girl (I wasn't about to do anything aggressive that would turn her off). I told her how much fun I had that night and she told me to call her soon.

Done and done, señorita! But first I had some skin cancer to tackle.

It was the week of my surgery. My mom had to stay home with Daniel, but my dad made the drive up from Winter Haven to be with me for the big day. We stayed up and chatted the night before the surgery, and my dad let me know that he had full faith that I would be cancer-free after the long day of surgery tomorrow. He also told me that countless people back home had been praying over me throughout the past couple of weeks, and there was a feeling of peace amongst them.

I wasn't that big into "hearing from God" at the time, but doggone it, I would take any good news I could get at this point. "Thanks, Dad," I said both appreciative and somewhat skeptical.

The next morning we headed off to St. Joseph's Hospital. They got me into my nice backless hospital gown (the standard dress code for people about to go under the knife), and then gave us our own private little room. Now my dad and I were waiting for someone to come get us.

"You nervous?" Dad asked.

"Heck yeah I'm nervous!" I almost shouted. "All I have been thinking about over the past few weeks is what if the cancer has spread? What if I lose my arm? How will I type and get things done quickly? Or what if I have to miss work for chemo treatment?" This was my first and only sick day in seven years, and money was clearly the driving factor in my life at the time.

"You are going to be just fine, Joe," my dad replied in his normal calm and collected manner.

Twenty minutes later they were wheeling me around in a wheelchair (probably so my butt wouldn't be showing to the world through my backless hospital gown) to see an interventional radiologist. He was tasked with looking at a few of my lymph nodes before they were taken out.

This was definitely the most painful part of the surgery, as I was awake, but it wasn't long before the doctor said he was done. He helped me back into the wheelchair, and he went to open the door for my dad and I so we could go back to our waiting room.

Then the weirdest and most unexpected thing happened. All of a sudden the doctor stopped dead in his tracks with his hand on the door. He turned around and looked at me, and said he felt he was being called to talk to me.

I glanced over at my dad wondering what the heck was going on. The doctor took a couple of steps toward me. At this point, I seriously didn't know if this guy was a crackpot or what.

He came over next to me and said, "I'm not legally supposed to do this, and I could potentially even get fired for this, but I feel the Lord asking me to pray over you. Do you mind if I pray for you?"

I glanced again at my dad, who looked as shocked as I did. All I could muster was, "Yes."

The doctor kneeled down next to my wheelchair, laid his hand on my right arm where the cancer was, and started praying. While he prayed out loud, I was trying desperately to hold in the tears. Too late… I began to weep. My dad began to cry too. The doctor kept praying over me.

After a few minutes of prayer he said, "Amen." He slowly stood back up, walked back to the door, and then turned around and looked at me. He said, "You have nothing to worry about son."

I gave him one last smile through my tear-soaked face. It was right there, in that moment, that I truly said, "Yes" to Jesus. I had always grown up a Christian, but I had never felt his presence or truly accepted him into my life until that day. I had never felt HIS energy running through my body like that before.

Now it's important to mention that at this point in my life I was not regularly attending church (minus the occasional Easter Sunday and Christmas service), and there had been zero mention of my beliefs, prayer, or anything related to being a Christian while in the room with this doctor that day. When he touched my arm it felt like electricity entering my body. From that day forward I was convinced of the power of *faith*, prayer, and the amazing energy that exists in this universe.

Back in our private waiting room my dad and I looked at each other, talked about the powerful moment we just experienced, and both started crying again. I was at complete peace with this cancer for the first time since the day the nurse came into my cubicle to deliver the terrible news.

Why?

I had God on my team now, and I knew it. Heck, I could even feel it. That day forever changed my faith, it changed how I prayed, and it completely altered my impression of faith-based thinking. Yes, I had read in several books about how powerful religious belief can be, but it took this unforeseen event in the hospital to hammer it home for me. It also changed my experience with God. This whole time I thought the only time I could speak to God or feel his presence was at church. Boy was I wrong. I had something in me that day. Some might call it the "Holy Spirit." Some might call it "energy from the universe." I'm still not sure what it was, but I know it wasn't a coincidence.

As I sat there in the waiting room thinking about all of the crazy things that had happened to me in the past thirty days, I began to believe that there were some invisible and very real forces at play in my life.

First of all there was the random guy on the airplane whom I was trying my best to avoid. If he had not told me to see a dermatologist that day I probably would have waited another year or two because I was so "busy" with work. If I had waited that long, the outcome could have been much worse (and potentially even resulted in death).

Then there was the nurse, who risked her job to have her nurse friend track me down and give me her phone number. She could have been fired if I had reported the incident. Had she not given me her number, I would not have been at the Braves game that Friday night where I happened to run into that beautiful blonde girl (the blonde girl's name was Loren and I ended up marrying her – my mom's "prophesy" came true).

Lastly there was this doctor, who also risked being reprimanded or even fired for praying over a random patient, whom he had just met, because he said he felt God's calling.

Not to mention if I hadn't been working in a building where there happened to be a dermatologist, I might have just put the whole thing off and none of this would have happened.

After seven excruciating days of waiting for all of the biopsies to come back (I had a huge chunk of my forearm removed along with three lymph nodes to see if the cancer had spread), I got the phone call from the doctor.

They were able to remove all of the cancer and the lymph nodes came back negative for melanoma. It was one of the best phone calls I had ever received, and I sat there and wept for a minute, gave some thanks to God, and decided it was time to start making some changes in my life.

HAVE FAITH.

The word faith is used over 240 times in the Bible. Faith is at the root of all modern-day miracles, and almost every personal development book that I have read has mentioned how critical FAITH is to your happiness.

Now, I want to point out that there are two types of faith that I believe are essential for your overall happiness. The great news is that they tie into one another.

The first is faith in a higher power. Faith in God. Faith in prayer. Faith in something bigger than ourselves. Now my intention is not to turn this book into a "religious book," but I firmly believe from all of my reading that it is tough to be happy and fulfilled if you don't have faith in some higher power and/or an unwavering belief system. Without faith, it's tough to have hope. Without hope, it's tough to have happiness.

If you've read one of the best-selling business books of all time, ***Think and Grow Rich***, by Napoleon Hill, you may recall that prayer, faith, and a burning desire around a thought is the crux of the book. Faith makes things happen. I have found that to be true in my personal and business life time and time again. Want to hit a goal? Then simply write it down, read it twice daily, have FAITH and BELIEVE you can achieve it, and then have a burning desire to hit the goal no matter what. You will be shocked at how your subconscious mind goes to work for you. I have had the craziest doors open in my life seemingly out of nowhere as a result of faith and a burning desire to hit a goal that I thought about every day.

One of the most inspiring stories about the power of faith and prayer is in ***Think and Grow Rich.*** It is the story of Napoleon's own son, who was born without ears. Doctors told him his son would be deaf his entire life.

But Napoleon had faith and spent time every single day praying for his son and telling him over and over that he was going to be able to hear one day. Napoleon continued to pray, continued to have blind faith, and continued to speak encouraging words to his son for over four years. His faith was relentless.

Napoleon's son would go on to hear almost as well as any other teenager. He was able to attend college and lead a normal life all because of Napoleon's faith that God can provide miracles. According to the book, it is the only case of a person being born without ears, who was able to hear normally in all of history (at the time).

Still not sure about having faith in God or some higher power? One of the most common things I hear from some of my friends (and quite honestly what I questioned a few times in my life) is how can I have "blind faith" in something that I have never seen? Or how can I afford to give so much of my life and thoughts to something I can't see, feel, or talk to?

My answer. How can you afford not to? How can you live your entire life believing that you are just a random occurrence, that you have no real purpose, that there is no higher power, and that you don't matter in this world?

I always find it so interesting that someone will have blind faith that a lightbulb will automatically come on when they flick a switch on the wall, but they won't believe that a higher power exists. You can't see the electricity, yet we all have faith every single day that it should work (and get really upset when it doesn't). We have faith that our laptops and phones will effortlessly sync up to some invisible Wi-Fi signal without having any clue how it all really works. We'll walk into an elevator and trust that it won't plummet to the bottom. If you look at it that way, faith is something we all put into practice on a daily basis whether we're aware of it or not.

Is it that much of a stretch, then, to believe that there is a higher power, that we were born for a reason, that God has big plans for us, and that we were meant to be fulfilled and happy?

I don't know about you, but the thought that we are only alive as a result of a completely random event, that the heavens don't exist, that there is no God above that loves us, and that faith can't move mountains is borderline depressing. Why does anything really matter if there is no God, no Creator, and no higher power than you and me?

There have even been extensive studies on how a religious faith can have massive impacts on a healthier and happier life. For instance, one study comparing elderly women with hip surgery revealed that the women with strong religious beliefs were able to walk farther after the hip surgery than women who didn't have religious beliefs. Furthermore, the study found that the religious women were also less depressed after surgery.

Interestingly, a study conducted by **Dr. Thomas Oxman** at Dartmouth Medical School found that religious patients over the age of fifty-five, who went through open-heart surgery for coronary or heart valve disease were three times (300%) more likely to survive the surgery than patients who had no faith.

I think the results of these studies stem from a particularly powerful element of faith; the belief that you're being cared for and that everything is going to be okay. When you feel assured that your life is in capable hands (whether it's God, the universe, or a benevolent force) it can be easier to "go with the flow" even as you step forward into the unknown.

Author **Michael Singer** refers to faith as a "surrender experiment" in his book by the same name. He notes the awesome and unexpected places he has been by giving into faith:

> *"For the lack of a better name, I have called this 'the surrender experiment,' and to the best of my ability, I have devoted the last forty years of my life to seeing where the flow of life's events would naturally take me. What happened over the course of these four decades is nothing short of phenomenal. Not only did things not fall apart, quite the opposite happened. As one thing naturally followed the other, the flow of life's events led me on a journey that would have been beyond my comprehension."*

It's that willingness to move forward in spite of uncertainty and "go with the flow," which I believe really enables us to achieve great things. As **Martin Luther King Jr.** said, *"Faith is taking the first step even when you don't see the whole staircase."*

The second type of faith is having faith in yourself. Behind every successful, happy, and fulfilled person is someone who believed in himself or herself.

I have yet to read a biography about a successful person or any self-help/personal development book in which the person says they didn't believe they could accomplish their lofty goals. Nope. In every story the subject had faith that they could achieve their goals, faith that they could be happy, and faith that they could get everything they wanted out of life. This type of faith is a mix of positive thinking, persistence, positive mental attitude, loving oneself, and action. If you don't believe in yourself no one else will.

Don't forget that your brain is very powerful. You have the power through your belief and faith to achieve what you set out to do. As Joseph Murphy reminds us in **The Power Of Your Subconscious Mind**, *"If you remain faithful to your mental attitude, your prayer will be answered."* It might not happen overnight, but if you stay focused on the things you want, you will eventually attain them.

The very first chapter in the book, **The Power Of Positive Thinking**, sums it up well with this quote: *"Believe in yourself! Have faith in your abilities! Without a humble but reasonable confidence in your own powers you cannot be successful or happy."*

A big part of finding happiness is **believing** you can have it and **knowing** you deserve it. As you grow in your journey with happiness don't forget the power of FAITH. As is promised to us in **Mark 9:23**: *"All things are possible for one who believes."* The next step is looking for the things you expect to find. Faith, as it turns out, is not a passive act.

FAITH IN LISTENING: THE POWER OF PRAYER AND SILENCE

The final recurring theme in many of the books I read was the power of prayer. Some books, like **The Surrender Experiment** by Michael Singer, refer to prayer as meditation or silent time used to tap into the energy of the universe. Likewise, **The Power Of Now** by Norman Vincent Peale and **The Purpose Driven Life** by Rick Warren mention prayer as the key to getting all that you want out of life.

Norman Vincent Peale said this about using prayer and meditation to get more energy and happiness out of life: *"God is the source of all energy - energy in the universe, atomic energy, electrical energy, and spiritual energy; indeed, every form of energy derives from the Creator."*

Similarly, author Eckhart Tolle spends a good chunk of his popular book, **The Power Of Now**, discussing why silence is so critical to happiness. Here is what he says: *"Pay more attention to the silence than to the sounds. Paying attention to outer silence creates inner silence: the mind becomes still. A* *portal is opening up... Every sound is born out of silence, dies back into silence, and during its life span is surrounded by silence. The Unmanifested (aka God) is present in this world as silence. This is why it has been said that nothing in this world is so like God as silence."*

Finally, numerous books, such as **Think And Grow Rich** and **The Master Key System** make mention of our brains and minds being compared to batteries. They also both say that the more brains/minds that are focused in prayer or in thought on a single problem, the more power they will have to solve it. My favorite quote on this was from **The Power Of Positive Thinking**:

"In our brains we have about two billion little storage batteries. The human brain can send off power by thoughts and prayers. The human body's magnetic power has actually been tested. We have thousands of little sending stations, and when these are turned up by prayer it is possible for a tremendous power to flow through a person and to pass between human beings. We can send off power by prayer which acts as both a sending and receiving station."

In **Think And Grow Rich** Hill expressed similar views:

"Faith is the head chemist of the mind. When faith is blended with thought, the subconscious mind instantly picks up the vibration, translates it into its spiritual equivalent, and transmits it to Infinite Intelligence, as in the case of prayer... you may convince the subconscious mind that you believe you will receive that for which you ask, and it will act upon that belief, which your subconscious mind passes back to you in the form of "faith," followed by definite plans for procuring that which you desire."

It's no wonder that one of the most quoted scriptures in the **Bible** on faith is on the power of faith and prayer:

"Have faith in God," Jesus said to them. Truly I tell you that if anyone says to this mountain, "Be lifted up and thrown into the sea," and has no doubt in his heart but believes that it will happen, it will be done for him. Therefore I tell you, whatever you ask in prayer, believe that you have received it, and it will be yours."

That goes for happiness and fulfillment too.

YOU'LL NEVER BE TRULY FULFILLED WITHOUT FAITH IN YOUR LIFE.

Faith in a higher power combined with faith in yourself is incredibly critical to long-term fulfillment. If you don't believe in some sort of higher power, calling, or sense that you are here for a reason, then why does anything really matter? Certainly you must have faith in yourself in order to grow spiritually and emotionally.

In ***Think And Grow Rich***, Napoleon Hill says, *"Have faith in yourself and faith in the Infinite. Faith is the "eternal elixir" which gives life, power, and action to the impulse of thought!"*

Pa-POW!

16

Why Positive Thinking Is
Useless Without Action

IT WAS THE first week of December 2011 and Loren and I were living in Houston, Texas. We were finally getting into a routine after having our first daughter, Shauna, a few months earlier. Since my wife didn't get much time off for maternity leave, she had to burn through all of her vacation and sick days just to get five weeks at home with our newborn daughter.

Now, with no vacation days left, Loren was practically working seven days a week. The rare day she did get off was usually spent catching up on sleep or studying. As you can imagine, I spent a lot of time with our baby daughter. In fact, it would be safe to say that I had very few friends or social engagements while in Houston. Although I regret not getting out much during this period (as it was a lonely couple of years), all of the time to myself did give me an opportunity to do one thing: read.

I had been a fairly consistent reader ever since an administrator at my high school named Bruce Downs gifted me my first book (Clive Cussler's *Cyclops*), and told me reading was cool. I looked up to him, so I gave it a try and actually enjoyed it. It probably helped that the action-hero Dirk Pitt from Cussler's books is one of the coolest dudes ever created in fiction (Dirk is basically James Bond for boating/fishing/ocean enthusiasts).

Now, years later, I was reading more personal development and business books than anything else. From Brian Tracey to Zig Ziglar to Tony Robbins to Malcolm Gladwell to Harvey Mackay, I couldn't get enough of these motivational books. I also felt like I was starting to develop my mind in new ways.

In one of his books Zig Ziglar talks about the power of growing your mind, learning a new word every day, and why reading new books is so critical to your growth. It became clear to me that although I was a pretty good reader, I still had so many books that I wanted to read and so much to learn. Zig's book also mentioned how he was reading one book per week, and I figured why couldn't I do that?

So I decided *not* to get an iPad…

You see, earlier that afternoon I had received a text from Loren asking me what I wanted for Christmas. "Mom needs to know, so just tell me what you want," she typed. I knew from the past that her parents usually spent anywhere from $100 to $150 on me every year. I also knew that I really wanted the new Apple iPad 2 which had just been released in March. So I did what many of us do and requested funds that I could put toward the new, expensive toy. But now I was having second thoughts after reading that Zigler book. Besides, this was during a very "unfulfilled" time in my life and my conscious was telling me that more books could be the answer I was looking for.

That night I told Loren I had changed my mind, and I wanted Amazon gift cards from everyone instead. I was going to buy nothing but books.

"What about your iPad?" my wife asked.

"iPads can't make me money," I replied. "Books can. I'm buying as many new sales, marketing, and personal development books as I can.

The day after Christmas I was counting up all of my Amazon gift cards. In total, I had $500 of Amazon gift cards to spend. Pa-POW! Now came the moment where the rubber meets the road… would I have the self-control to actually spend it all on books?

Shortly after New Year's boxes began hitting my doorstep. I believe I ordered close to thirty books over the course of just a couple months. Most notable was the fact that I ordered TWELVE Dan Kennedy books. From his No B.S. books to *Make 'Em Laugh & Take Their Money* to his "uncensored" book with Sydney Barrows, I was going to engross myself in reading.

If you can believe it, by the end of March, I had read every one of the Dan Kennedy books I bought. I averaged at least one new book per week for the twelve-week stretch. Were they impactful? Let's just say that I later told my in-laws I turned their $150 Amazon gift card into $100,000. And that is probably being conservative.

How did I take twelve books and turn them into $100,000? It's pretty simple really. I read them, I took notes, I dog-eared pages, and then I took **ACTION**!

My goal was the same for every book. Find the one takeaway point that could impact my life and/or current job and take action on it. Not ten big takeaways, not five, not two, but ONE. Then I worked on making it happen in my life. I did that twelve times (one big idea implemented from each book) and all of a sudden I started making more money than I ever had in my life. In fact, the next year I almost made double the amount of my previous highest income. I still recall the rush of making $100,000 in a single month for the first time, and I knew much of that new wealth was from these books I had read.

Over the next couple of years I bought countless online courses from everything on how to get my YouTube videos to show up on the top spot, to how to create irresistible offers and sales letters, to how to build on-line funnels. I was reading at breakneck speed and probably spent at least $50,000 on courses and books.

Do you know what I found to be true for every single dollar that I spent, every single course I purchased, and every single book I read? I figured out that none of it mattered much unless I took ACTION with what I learned. It is a common misconception that knowledge equals power. I say hogwash! All of the education and knowledge in the world has little to no value if it can't be harnessed, organized, and used. In other words, if you know how to do something, but you never actually DO it or share it with someone else, then is it worth much? I don't think so.

One of the biggest eye-openers I had with all of this self-help stuff was when I went to my first Brendon Burchard conference near Silicon Valley. Earlier that year I had purchased one of Brendon's online courses for approximately $2,000. With the online course came a couple of awesome bonuses, including two free tickets to one of Brendon's live events.

I took my brother Luke with me, and when we got to the conference room that morning I was blown away by the energy from the 800+ people in the room. Surrounded by such bright, motivated people, I was starting to feel a bit inadequate. I started telling myself that these people must be some of the top businessmen and entrepreneurs in the country. I was shocked when I found out the truth.

After the wild intro/dance party was over Brendon started going into his lesson for the first day. At first, it appeared that he was simply regurgitating parts of the online course, which most everyone in the room had purchased months before. I thought to myself that surely Brendon was just doing an overview or refresher of the course. However, an hour later, he was still going through the same material that I had just gone through at home. Two hours later... still nothing new. I started whispering to my brother, "He's literally just going through the same thing he just sold us." Four hours later he was still on the course, and I looked around to see almost every person in the room feverishly taking notes like they had never heard this stuff before.

It turns out that Brendon knew something that I didn't know. It was that a tiny portion of people who buy online courses actually finish them. In fact, most people never start them! Here is what happens. They purchase the course, then fool themselves into thinking they have solved the problem because they now "own the solution." Their happiness goes up. Their anxiety goes down. All because they believe that they've resolved the issue that they were trying to overcome! Of course, we all know that eventually they come down from the artificial high (as they never even started the course), and end up exactly where they started.

This isn't something new. All of the gurus and online marketers are in the same boat with their tribes. I overheard Internet marketer Frank Kern say something that couldn't be more true, though very few online marketers would ever say so. Frank said that most people don't need another self-help course. What they really need is to go and finish the last couple that they purchased and never started.

Then I was really in for a shock. The following day of the Brendon Burchard event we got into a bunch of little groups with many of the strangers sitting around us. I got to meet some amazing people from all kinds of industries and backgrounds. As I began meeting these people, I started asking everyone if they had started the online course they purchased. One by one they admitted they hadn't, or that they had started the first module and decided "to get back to it later" after the event.

My next question to all of the new people I was meeting was if they had created their first information product yet (the same thing they had paid $2,000 to learn how to do many months earlier). One by one gave me an excuse on why they hadn't. Thankfully, I did finally meet some people who not only had created their info courses but were making more money than me. We seemed to be the only action-takers, and not coincidentally, we were the ones who had seen the most benefit from Brendon's great advice (side note: Brendon eventually got into some new material that wasn't in the course, and I highly encourage everyone to attend at least one of his events. They are pretty amazing).

What's the moral of the story?

TAKE ACTION!

You aren't going to find happiness by procrastinating, sitting on the couch (it's proven that moderate TV usage does NOT increase happiness and too much TV decreases happiness in your life), or wishing and praying for things to happen. You have to take action to see the change you want in your life. You have to act to see miracles. As **Dan Kennedy** says, "*ACT FIRST.*" That means don't wait for anyone or anything that is getting in the way of your happiness or success. Just do it.

In Ryan Holiday's **The Obstacle Is The Way,** he takes a look at the Roman Emperor Marcus Aurelius' life. Do you know what Marcus Aurelius said were the three most powerful words? They were, *"Action, Action, Action."*

Kamal Ravikant said something almost identical in his book, ***Live Your Truth***, when he talked about finding your mission in life. Here is what he said:

> *"There is a secret. To life, to love, to living your truth, to success in anything… the secret is this: pick something that is important to you. One thing. Look at your belief on it, what you know to be true. Then, as if diving off a board, your feet already in the air, you commit…"* and then,

"Do the work. Do the work. Do the work. Do the work. Do the work.

Do. The. Work."

Far too many people go through life waiting for the "right time" before they take action. And far too many people say, "I'll do it when _____ happens," or, "I'll start it after _____." It's no surprise that many of these same people scratch their head wondering why they aren't happy.

A great quote on this subject is from the book, ***The Science Of Getting Rich***, by Wallace D. Wattles. Here is what Wallace said about never waiting to take action: *"Do not wait for a change of environment before you act; get a change of environment by action. Do not spend any time day dreaming or castle building; hold to the one vision of what you want, and act Now."* These words were written almost 100 years ago and still hold true today.

You can do anything in life if you set a goal, write it down, take action, and stop making excuses. Act First! And if you can't act first, then at least act second. The worst thing you can do is not take any action when you know you should.

Don't be like most people that never finish what they set out to do. Or even worse, the huge percentage of people that never even start. Too many people get excited about something, start the first module or chapter, get distracted with "life," promise themselves they will pick it back up next week and never touch it again only to wonder why they still have the problem they wanted to solve. Don't be that person. It is incredibly tough to find happiness and achieve things without taking action.

You can have all of the positive thinking and motivation in the world, but if you never take action on anything, it won't matter. A Ferrari full of gas will go nowhere if it stays in the garage. In Neil Pasricha's ***The***

Happiness Equation, he says, *"Motivation doesn't cause action. Action causes motivation."* You can't think your way into getting things done.

In Wallace D. Wattles' ***The Science Of Getting Rich***, he says, *"By thought you can cause the gold in the hearts of the mountains to be impelled toward you; but it will not mine itself, coin itself into double eagles, and come rolling along the roads seeking its way into your pocket."*

All of the self-help books I have read agree on one thing:

No Action = No Happiness.

Former British Prime Minister Benjamin Disraeli famously said, *"Action may not always bring happiness, but there is no happiness without action."*

One of my favorite Dan Kennedy quotes on action is from his book, ***The Ultimate Marketing Plan***, where he says, *"There are three types of people: those who make things happen, those who watch things happen, and those who wonder what happened. I think you'll find that most successful people are in the first category."*

Phil Knight's story about how he created Nike from nothing in his book, ***Shoe Dog***, is a great example of what Kennedy is talking about. Phil shares a time in his life where he was dead broke and trying to decide if he should fold his struggling shoe company and get a "normal job" or keep going. He decided to make something happen and take action toward the thing that would bring him fulfillment:

"The whole thing might go bust any day, but I still couldn't see myself doing anything else. My little shoe company was a living, breathing thing, which I'd created from nothing.

"I flat out didn't want to work for someone else. I wanted to build something that was my own, something I could point to and say: I MADE that. It was the only way I saw to make life meaningful."

As we talked about earlier in the book, don't let fear make you think you are taking the wrong action. You will fail at some point, and there is nothing wrong with that. Eckhart Tolle has this to say about risking failure in the name of action in **The Power Of Now**:

"Any action is often better than no action, especially if you have been stuck in an unhappy situation for a long time. If it is a mistake, at least you learn something, in which case it's no longer a mistake. If you remain stuck, you learn nothing. Is fear preventing you from taking action? Acknowledge the fear, watch it, take your attention into it, be fully present with it. Doing so cuts the link between the fear and your thinking."

I also tell you all of this to make sure your mind is ready and prepared for what you will have to do. If you don't take action, then you won't see a huge transformation. The great news is that if you have made it this far, you are already farther ahead than most people. Countless people will buy this book and never even open up the first page. They are the same ones who wonder why they can't find happiness in their life. On the other hand, every single successful, fulfilled, and happy person I have studied got to where they are through steady and consistent hourly, daily, weekly, monthly, and annual action (aka productivity).

Bradley Whitford tells us that anything is truly possible with action: *"Infuse your life with action. Don't wait for it to happen. Make it happen. Make your own future. Make your own hope. Make your own love. And whatever your beliefs, honor your creator, not by passively waiting for grace to come down from upon high, but by doing what you can to make grace happen... yourself, right now, right down here on Earth."*

Your happiness and fulfillment are within your capacity to create. Provided, of course, that you actually do it. Start right now.

Take Action.

Implement.

Grow.

Be Happy.

Action
Summary/*Action* Steps

WITH THE RIGHT attitude, a burning desire to be happy, and the determination to take action, pretty much anything you set out to accomplish is possible. Have you heard the story about how **Sylvester Stallone** went from being practically homeless with no job to starring in *Rocky*, a movie that he wrote in twenty hours? It's the ultimate story of knowing what you stand for, having the right attitude, and taking massive action to make it happen.

Ever since Sylvester Stallone was a young man he knew that he wanted to be in the movie business. Not just behind the scenes or working a camera; he wanted to play a part in movies. To Sylvester, the movies were the ultimate way for him to inspire and move massive amounts of people, and he knew that this was his mission in life.

But Sylvester had a couple of things working against him. At birth he was pulled out by the forceps, which is the reason he talks a bit funny (he speaks out of the side of his mouth). Many of the casting agencies said that Sylvester "looked dopey" when he auditioned for roles in movies. He wasn't exactly the kind of male star that Hollywood wanted. To make matters worse, he had no experience and no connections in the movie business.

That didn't stop Sylvester from trying. He claims he was thrown out of nearly every single talent agency in New York. As he put it to Tony Robbins, he got tossed out of over 1,500 agency offices (there aren't that many in New York, but he was rejected and asked to leave each agency numerous times).

Sylvester and his wife were barely able to pay their bills, and he was eventually forced to sell almost everything in their apartment just to keep the heat on during one cold winter. He hit a new low when he took his wife's jewelry and sold them off to pay for food. Needless to say, it is no surprise he spent a few nights outside like a homeless man during this period.

He and his wife fought constantly. She didn't understand why he wouldn't give up his dumb dream of being in the movies and just get a real job. Sylvester knew that if he got a "real job," then he would most likely give up on his life's mission to inspire people as a movie star.

He eventually started to write movie scripts so he could sell them and make some money while he continued to audition for roles. After countless rejections, he sold his first script for $100. Now that might not seem like a lot when you consider the time that goes into writing a full movie script, but when you don't have a single dollar to your name $100 is a fortune.

As you can imagine that money went fast, and they ran completely out of cash again. Sylvester recalls hitting rock bottom. It was at this time in his life that he had no other choice than to sell his best friend, his dog Butkus. He sold his dog for a measly $25 to a guy outside of a liquor store, who negotiated him down from $100.

According to Sylvester, this was the low point in his life. He was almost about to give up. Just days later while watching a fight between Mohammed

Ali and an underdog named Chuck Wepner (Chuck went a full fifteen rounds with the champ after taking an absolute beating), Sylvester stayed up that night and wrote the entire script for *Rocky* in twenty hours.

He knew this was his big break, but after pitching it to numerous production groups, all he heard were things like, "It's too predictable," "It's stupid," and, "It's sappy." (He later read all of these negative comments at the Oscars when he won all of his awards for the movie).

Finally, one group liked the script and ended up offering him $125,000 for it! This was more money than he had seen in his lifetime. There was just one problem: Sylvester wanted to play Rocky, and they wanted a well-known actor, not some unknown writer.

They argued back and forth, and eventually they told Sylvester to take the $125,000 cash offer or leave it. He left their office with the script in his hand and no money to show for it.

The group called him a few weeks later and doubled their offer. They would pay him a staggering $250,000 for his script if he agreed not to star in his movie. After more back and forth, he walked out again. They eventually came back with their final offer; $325,000 for him to sell the script and get on with life. He said no. He wasn't giving up the rights to the movie unless he played Rocky Balboa.

They finally made a compromise and gave him $35,000 plus part ownership in the movie royalties (as they didn't think it would work). They told him they weren't going to spend a lot of money on if he was going to play the lead role in the movie.

Can you guess the first thing he did when he received his $35,000? He went down to the liquor store to see if he could find the guy that bought his dog for $25. He was going to buy Butkus back. After two days of searching, he began to think he would never see Butkus again. However, on the third day, he finally saw the two out in front of the liquor store.

He rushed up to the man and offered to pay the guy his $25 back. The man refused. Sylvester then offered the guy $500.

"No way," the guy said. "He is my dog now, and you can't buy him back."

He offered the guy $1,000 for Butkus, and still the man said no. "No amount of money is going to buy this dog back," the man replied.

Nothing was going to stop Sylvester from getting what he wanted. $15,000 and a part in his movie later, Sylvester had his best friend Butkus back. The group that bought Sylvester's script ended up spending a mere $1 million to make the original Rocky. It went on to win numerous awards and grossed over $200,000,000! According to sources familiar with the deal, Sylvester owned 10%. Butkus and the guy who bought him for $25 can be seen in the movie as extras. Pretty awesome.

As you probably know, Sylvester went on to star in tons of movies over the years and now gets millions to play lead roles. All of this despite talking out of the side of his mouth and looking "dopey." He never gave up on his life's mission, and it paid off handsomely.

Attitude can change your life. Or, as **Rocky Balboa** says, "*Until You Start Believing In Yourself, You Ain't Gonna Have A Life.*"

Many people have said "Attitude is everything, " but I disagree. The truth is that **"Attitude + Action = Everything."** You can wake up and smile all day long, but if you don't get off your bum and make something happen, you are just a stick figure with a big smile. You won't get the results you want by simply faking it. You can have the best attitude in the world, but if you don't do anything with it then it's somewhat meaningless.

This fourth and final cornerstone is one of the easiest to do, yet hardest to master. It's easy to take a little bit of action and stay positive for a day or two. It's also easy to take action now and then. However, it's incredibly hard to be consistent at both taking action and having a great attitude. For those who can do both consistently… the world is yours.

YOUR *ACTION* STEPS:

1. Start believing that everything happens for a reason and know that **happiness is a choice**.
2. Write down goals and take massive action every day to achieve them.
3. Know that life is happening FOR you and not TO you.
4. Wake up every morning thankful to be alive.
5. Set realistic expectations (goals too big can leave you frustrated and goals too small aren't challenging and fulfilling).
6. Have FAITH in a higher power and in yourself.
7. If you have a family, replicate the daily ritual that the "Life Is Good" mother did with her family and ask, *"tell me something good that happened today."*
8. Change the way you see the world. Change how you see yourself.
9. Pray.
10. Take ACTION!

Section 4

Happiness Concluded

17

Will You Have These Same Regrets When You Die?

"On one hand, we all want to be happy. On the other hand, we all know the things that make us happy. But we don't do those things. Why? Simple. We are too busy. Too busy doing what? Too busy trying to be happy…"

MATTHEW KELLY'S WORDS really strike a chord with me. Have you ever asked yourself, "Is this the best my life is going to get? Or "How did my life turn out so much different than I imagined?" Or "This isn't where I thought I would be at this point in my life?" How about, "I sure thought I would be happier than this now that I _____ (have a nice paying job, own a new home, got married, had my first child, graduated high school, etc.)."

As kids we all have these dreams about what we are going to do and be when we grow up. When we DO finally get older we rarely find ourselves doing what we imagined as kids. We feel disappointed.

Well, the good news is that you are not alone if you find yourself thinking like this from time to time. It turns out that nearly all adults have had these thoughts at one moment or another. I know I sure have. It's only normal to look back on your life and wonder how you got to where you are now. It's perfectly understandable to look back at missed opportunities and wonder what might have been. However, when you look back and feel intense regret, that's a different story.

No one knows that better than Bronnie Ware.

If you haven't heard of Bronnie Ware before, don't worry, neither had I before I read her eye-opening story. Bronnie is an Australian hospice nurse who spent many years caring for patients in the last three to twelve weeks of their lives. In other words, she worked with people who knew they were going to die in the next couple of months. She spoke candidly with them every day as they watched their last days go by.

One question she asked every one of her dying patients was if they had any regrets in life or what, if anything, they would do differently. Over the years she listened, took notes, cried with her patients, and finally shared her findings.

Here are the top five things that her dying patients told her they wished they had done differently in life:

REGRET #1: I WISH I'D HAD THE COURAGE TO LIVE A LIFE TRUE TO MYSELF, NOT THE LIFE OTHERS EXPECTED OF ME.

According to Bronnie this was the number one regret. Many people do things just to please others, rather than staying true to themselves. What's sad is to think about how many dreams have gone unfulfilled because we tried to live up to others' expectations. Don't have this regret. Do what makes you happy. Never do it for someone else; not even your parents, spouse, or boss.

REGRET #2: I WISH I DIDN'T WORK SO HARD.

This is probably not a shocker, but no one on their deathbed sits there wishing that they had spent more time in the office. In fact, it is something that most people regret. Something they wish they could go back and change.

Most of us spend the vast majority of our adult lives working (whether you are in an office, on the road, on a plane, or working from home). Now with "tools" like smartphones and laptops, we are expected to respond to emails pretty much around the clock. The line between work and personal/family time has blurred so badly that it's tough to know how much time we spend working. What is certainly clear is that we all work too much. Isn't it ironic that we have more timesaving devices, apps, and gadgets than ever, yet we are all more stressed out and never feel like we have enough time?

As if working too much and feeling like you never have enough time isn't bad enough… the worst part is most people work too hard doing jobs they don't love. I'm no career expert, but I am smart enough to know that God never intended his children to spend the majority of their waking hours doing things they hate.

REGRET #3: I WISH I'D HAD THE COURAGE TO EXPRESS MY FEELINGS.

Guilty as charged. This one hit me right in between the eyes.

The only way to have a healthy and rewarding relationship with anyone (friends, parents, sibling, child, boss, neighbor, etc.) is to be able to speak honestly and openly with them. If you are holding back your feelings, you won't develop the kind of relationships that you seek.

This regret also applies to holding grudges, being resentful, talking behind people's backs, and more. There are even stories of people becoming incredibly sick and unhealthy due to holding on to resentment and hate. It's impossible for your mind to grow and flourish if it is being held back with negativity and hatred. Period.

It's not just about letting go of anger or resentment. It's also about telling the people you love how much you love them and making sure they know that they're important to you. THAT is the part that smacked me in the face. It made me think of my dad.

I'm not sure how it happened, but for as long as I can remember, my dad and I have never really told each other that we love each other. We both certainly do. My mom and I say we love each other regularly, but with my dad it's different. I feel like we both want to say it, but the words just never come out.

After two decades of uncomfortable silence neither of us has taken the initiative to just say it. Since this is a common regret, I am certain my dad and I are not alone on this.

Dad, I know you are reading this, and I want to tell you something publicly so you never doubt it...

I love you.

REGRET #4: I WISH I HAD STAYED IN TOUCH WITH MY FRIENDS.

Have you ever thought about one of your best friends, realized that you hadn't spoken to them in ages, told yourself you would call them that day, only to get so caught up in your busy life that it slipped through the cracks?

I know I've been there way too many times. If you think you will regret not staying in touch with your friends when you are on your deathbed, then make it is a "must do" and not a "might do" going forward. It's not worth regretting later.

REGRET # 5: I WISH THAT I HAD LET MYSELF BE HAPPIER.

I was not shocked to see this regret on the list—in fact, I'm glad it's there. What this confirms is that happiness is a **CHOICE.**

Most of us get so caught up in ruts, bad habits, and boring daily patterns that we start to falsely think happiness isn't a choice. Nothing could be further from the truth.

Your Happiness Is A Choice.

Do you know what else?

YOU ARE A MIRACLE!

You are good looking.

You are loved.

You are a winner!

I believe that we all beat ourselves up way too much, and we spend way too much time comparing ourselves to others. It's no shock that we sometimes feel like we are failures. We are constantly comparing ourselves to someone else who is richer and better looking, or who has a nicer car, bigger home, better job, or whatever it might be.

Did you realize that from the day you were conceived you were a winner? Did you know that you outswam, outmaneuvered, and won a race against somewhere between 250 million and 1 billion others? That is like winning the Boston Marathon 50 years in row! The chances of getting struck by lighting are 1 in 700,000 per year, and you were the ONE in 250,000,000!

You were the absolute strongest. You were the leader of the pack in the most competitive "life or death" race of your life. You got LIFE while millions of your competitors died that day. Think about that for a second. You are a WINNER.

The good news is that your awesomeness doesn't end there! According to UNESCO, approximately 25% of the adult population in the world is illiterate. There is another 25% of the literate group that will not pick up a single book this year. So the fact that you are reading these words means you are smarter, more willing to learn, and more likely to be successful and happy than *billions* of people!

Just know this: God handpicked you out of hundreds of millions of other humans he could have given life to because he had a special plan for you. The big question you need to ask yourself as you read this book is are you living up to it? Is there room for improvement? Are you celebrating life like you just won a race where the odds were against you? You are a WINNER!!! You are a MIRACLE!!!

If you think God went to all of that trouble to create a miracle just to have you not be happy, not feel important, and never life a fulfilled life, then you are wrong. He wants nothing more than for you to succeed, be happy, be fulfilled, and to leave an amazing legacy. The same things you would want for your own children.

It's time to start celebrating your life.

Take the *Dalai Lama's* words to heart when he says, "*Every day, think as you wake up, 'Today I am fortunate to have woken up, I am alive, I have a precious human life, I am not going to waste it. I am going to use all my energies to develop myself, to expand my heart out to others. I am going to benefit others as much as I can."*

Pa-POW!

Final Thoughts: The Second Most Important Day Of Your Life

"Happiness is the meaning of life, the whole aim and end of human existence."

— ARISTOTLE

MY FATHER-IN-LAW HAS an old farmhouse in a small rural city called, Dublin, Georgia. The original farmhouse was built back around 1865, but after burning down many generations ago, it was rebuilt and stands looking pretty amazing today.

The farmhouse sits on approximately 500 acres of land. One of the things that my father-in-law did to help pay the big tax bills on the land was to plant pine trees on as many acres as he could.

One day he decided to drive me through the property to show me all of the trees he had planted. We first came up to the mature pine trees, and he told me how they would harvest the pine needles and sell them during the fall. He also informed me that he planted these trees over twenty years ago, and that the most valuable and strongest wood comes from twenty-five to thirty-five-year-old trees.

I asked him when he was planning on cutting these mature trees down and he said, "Joe, the beauty of trees like these is that if you take care of them and give them the nutrients that they need, they will pay for themselves from the needles they drop every year. Then you can wait until timber prices are where you want them to finally decide to harvest them."

He then showed me some of the newer trees, which stretched as far as I could see. They were thin and scrawny, and they couldn't have been much taller than me. It was hard to imagine that these small trees would look like the mature ones we saw earlier.

My father-in-law looked over the tops of these baby pine trees, and then he looked over at me and asked, "Joe, do you know the best time to plant a pine tree?"

I thought he was talking about what time of year, so I guessed the spring.

He looked at me with a grin and said, "No. The best time to plant a pine tree is twenty years ago."

We were both silent for a couple of seconds as I tried to digest what he was telling me.

He continued on, "Joe, do you know the second best time to plant a pine tree?"

I was silent this time to avoid looking any dumber.

"Today," he answered.

What a powerful statement. I haven't forgotten it since I heard it, as it applies to so many things in life.

The best time to lose weight and hit the gym is years ago, but the second best time is **TODAY.**

The best time to save money is years ago when you got your first paycheck, but the second best time is **TODAY.**

The best time to get over your fear of public speaking, anxiety attacks, or any other debilitating fear was back when they first occurred. The second best time is **TODAY.**

The best time to tell your mom, dad, wife, husband, or kids that you love them was years ago, but the second best time is **TODAY.**

The best time to be happy and fulfilled was years ago, but the second best time is **TODAY.**

The best time to declare your mission in life was years ago, but the second best time is **TODAY.**

Just like a pine tree needs time to grow and mature, fulfillment won't happen overnight. It will only happen if you take the right action and start planting the seeds **TODAY.**

The best news is that you have all of the pieces of the puzzle, and life is sure to give you more. More importantly, you have your four cornerstone pieces and you know exactly what the puzzle is supposed to look like. It's up to you to put it all together now. Start **TODAY.**

The most important day in your life was the day you were born. It was nothing short of a miracle that you came into this world. The day you were born was God breathing life into you. It was you feeling the rush of air through your body for the very first time. It was your very first day of your life's ever-changing jigsaw puzzle.

The second most important day is **TODAY**.

Every day you wake up able to breathe is a day that you can make a difference in your life and the life of others. Every day you wake up alive is a day you can **CHOOSE** to be happy and fulfilled. And regardless of who you are, how old you are, or what family you were born in, you deserve to be happy and fulfilled in life.

Finally, don't forget the third most important day in your life. It is the day you die. How will you be remembered on that day? What will your legacy be to the world? Will people say you just went through the motions and stayed in between the lines, or that you lived life to the fullest and made an impact? Will people talk about how you were only driven by material things and had few friends, or that you were loving, generous, and had countless friends? Will people know what your mission and purpose were in life? Will you die with the same regrets that most people have or be one of the few who can honestly say you spent your final days fulfilled?

IT'S YOUR CHOICE. AND YOU MUST TAKE ACTION.

I hope you enjoyed the book, and I hope you learned something from my stories and all of the books I have read and curated. I hope you realize that fulfillment is yours to be had, and I hope you know that it's time to finally stop fishing for happiness and start doing some serious catching.

Go Forth. Find your Purpose. Own your Fears. Dream BIG. Find Faith. Smile like it's your last day on Earth. Take Action. Live a Happy and Fulfilled life. Do it TODAY. You deserve nothing less.

~ Joe Simonds

P.S. – If you think a loved one, friend, family member, coworker, or neighbor could benefit from this book, please make sure to share a copy with them. If everyone lived with a purpose and found more happiness in their lives, this world would be a better place.

P.P.S. - If you really got a lot out of *Fishing For Happiness*, please head to *Amazon* and leave me a review on what you got out of the book. I read every single review, and I'd love to hear from you.

About The Author

JOE SIMONDS LIVES in Tampa, Florida with his amazing wife Loren and their three children (two girls and a boy). He is an avid fisherman, blogger, reader, beer taster, and chapstick addict. Joe and his brother Luke started the fishing apparel brands Salt Strong and Fish Strong, which continue to keep them busy as they try to disrupt the fishing world.

You can follow Joe's blog and "Happiness Updates" at www.joesimonds.com

You can follow Joe and Luke in their fishing exploits over at www.saltstrong.com and www.fishstrong.com

Notes & References:

If you want to see the Full Book List that I read and referenced to write Fishing For Happiness, then go to www.joesimonds.com/ffh-full-book-list

For a list of my "Must Read" books go to www.joesimonds.com/ffh-must-read-list

To subscribe to my weekly "Happiness" email newsletter and to be the first to see my new content every week, go to www.joesimonds.com and sign up for my FREE newsletter.

Made in the USA
Lexington, KY
09 April 2017